I0415862

August 2012

ENTREPRENEURIAL ASSISTANCE

Opportunities Exist to Improve Programs' Collaboration, Data-Tracking, and Performance Management

GAO
Accountability * Integrity * Reliability

Highlights

Highlights of GAO-12-819, a report to congressional committees

ENTREPRENEURIAL ASSISTANCE

Opportunities Exist to Improve Programs' Collaboration, Data-Tracking, and Performance Management

Why GAO Did This Study

Economic development programs that effectively provide assistance to entrepreneurs may help businesses develop and expand. GAO focused on 52 economic development programs, with an estimated $2.0 billion in funding, at Commerce, HUD, SBA, and USDA that support entrepreneurs. In response to a statutory requirement, this report discusses (1) the extent of overlap and fragmentation, the effects on entrepreneurs, and agencies' actions to address them; and (2) the extent of tracked program information and whether these programs have met their performance goals and been evaluated. To address these objectives, GAO analyzed program information and interviewed agency officials in headquarters and selected field offices, entrepreneurs, and third-party entities, such as nonprofits, that use federal grants to provide assistance directly to entrepreneurs.

What GAO Recommends

GAO recommends that the agencies and the Office of Management and Budget explore opportunities to enhance collaboration among programs, both within and across agencies; track program information; and conduct more program evaluations. Commerce, HUD, and USDA provided written comments and each neither agreed nor disagreed with the recommendations. However, USDA commented that the recommendations were not explicit. In the report, GAO provides specific actions that agencies can take to address each recommendation.

View GAO-12-819. For more information, contact William B. Shear at (202) 512-8678 or shearw@gao.gov.

What GAO Found

Federal efforts to support entrepreneurs are fragmented—including among 52 programs at the Department of Agriculture (USDA), Commerce, and Housing and Urban Development (HUD) and the Small Business Administration (SBA). All overlap with at least one other program in terms of the type of assistance they are authorized to offer, such as financial (grants and loans) and technical (training and counseling), and the type of entrepreneur they are authorized to serve. Some entrepreneurs struggle to navigate the fragmented programs that provide technical assistance. For example, some entrepreneurs and technical assistance providers GAO spoke with said the system can be confusing and that some entrepreneurs do not know where to go for assistance. Collaboration could reduce some negative effects of overlap and fragmentation, but field staff GAO spoke with did not consistently collaborate to provide training and counseling services to entrepreneurs. The agencies have taken initial steps to improve how they collaborate by entering into formal agreements, but they have not pursued a number of other good collaborative practices GAO has previously identified. For example, USDA and SBA entered into a formal agreement in 2010 to coordinate their efforts to support businesses in rural areas; however, the agencies' programs that can support start-up businesses—such as USDA's Rural Business Enterprise Grant program and SBA's Small Business Development Centers—have yet to determine roles and responsibilities, find ways to leverage each other's resources, or establish compatible policies and procedures. Without enhanced collaboration and coordination agencies may not be able to make the best use of limited federal resources in the most effective and efficient manner.

Agencies do not track program information on entrepreneurial assistance activities for many programs, a number of programs have not met their performance goals, and most programs lack evaluations. In particular, the agencies do not generally track information on the specific type of assistance they provide or the entrepreneurs they serve, in part because they do not rely on this information to administer the programs. Rather, agencies may rely, for example, on data summaries in narrative format, which cannot be easily aggregated or analyzed. According to government standards for internal control, this information should be available to help inform management in making decisions and identifying risks and problem areas. GAO also found that 19 programs failed to meet their annual performance goals related to entrepreneurial assistance, including USDA's Rural Business Opportunity Grants, Commerce's Economic Development/Support for Planning Organizations, HUD's Indian Community Development Block Grants, and SBA's 504 loans to finance commercial real estate. Programs could potentially rely on results from program evaluations to determine the reasons why they have not met their goals, as well as to gauge overall effectiveness. However, the agencies lack program evaluations for 32 of the 52 programs. Therefore, information on program efficiency and effectiveness is limited, and scarce resources may be going toward programs that are less effective. In addition, without more robust program information, agencies may not be able to administer programs in the most effective and efficient manner.

Contents

Tables

Figures

Abbreviations

BEDI	Brownfields Economic Development Initiative
CDBG	Community Development Block Grant
CDC	Community Development Corporation
CFDA	Catalog of Federal Domestic Assistance
Commerce	Department of Commerce
EDA	Economic Development Administration
FAST	Federal and State Technology Partnership
GPRA	Government Performance and Results Act
GPRAMA	GPRA Modernization Act of 2010
HUBZone	Historically Underutilized Business Zone
HUD	Department of Housing and Urban Development
MBC	Minority Business Center
MBDA	Minority Business Development Agency
NABEC	Native American Business Enterprise Centers
NMVC	New Markets Venture Capital
OMB	Office of Management and Budget
PRIME	Program for Investment in Micro-Entrepreneurs
SBA	Small Business Administration
SBDC	Small Business Development Center
SBIC	Small Business Investment Company
SBIR	Small Business Innovation Research
STTR	Small Business Technology Transfer
TAA	Trade Adjustment Assistance
USDA	U.S. Department of Agriculture
VAPG	Value Added Producer Grants
WBC	Women's Business Center

United States Government Accountability Office
Washington, DC 20548

August 23, 2012

Congressional Committees

Entrepreneurs play a vital role in the U.S. economy. The federal government provides a variety of support and assistance to them, and dozens of programs exist to support entrepreneurs across numerous federal agencies. Economic development programs that effectively provide assistance to entrepreneurs, in conjunction with state and local government and private sector economic development initiatives, may help businesses develop and expand. However, we have previously raised questions about the potential negative effects of fragmentation and overlap among federal programs that can support entrepreneurs. Specifically, we have questioned how efficiently federal agencies are administering these programs and how effective the programs are at achieving their mission. This report focuses on 52 programs administered by the U.S. Departments of Agriculture (USDA), Commerce (Commerce), and Housing and Urban Development (HUD) and the U.S. Small Business Administration (SBA) that provide assistance to entrepreneurs.[1] In 2011, we examined these programs and found that each program overlapped with at least one other program in terms of the economic development activities that they are authorized to fund.[2] According to agency officials, these programs, which typically fund a variety of activities in addition to supporting entrepreneurs, spent an estimated $2.0 billion on economic development efforts in fiscal year 2011.

Section 21 of Public Law 111-139, enacted in February 2010, requires GAO to conduct routine investigations to identify federal programs, agencies, offices, and initiatives with duplicative goals and activities within

---

[1]The number of programs administered by Commerce, HUD, SBA, and USDA that we identified in February 2012 as supporting entrepreneurial efforts decreased from 53 to 52 because USDA's Empowerment Zones program was ended by Congress during fiscal year 2010 and has been excluded from this review. See GAO, *2012 Annual Report: Opportunities to Reduce Duplication, Overlap and Fragmentation, Achieve Savings, and Enhance Revenue*, GAO-12-342SP (Washington, D.C.: Feb. 28, 2012).

[2]GAO, *Opportunities to Reduce Potential Duplication in Government Programs, Save Tax Dollars, and Enhance Revenue*, GAO-11-318SP (Washington D.C.: Mar. 1, 2011) and *Efficiency and Effectiveness of Fragmented Economic Development Programs Are Unclear*, GAO-11-477R (Washington, D.C.: May 19, 2011).

departments and governmentwide, and report annually to Congress.[3] This report discusses (1) the extent of overlap, fragmentation, and duplication and their effects on entrepreneurs, and agencies' actions to address them; and (2) the extent to which agencies collect information necessary to track program activities and whether these programs have met their performance goals and have been evaluated.

While we identified a more comprehensive list of federal programs that can fund economic activities more generally, we focused our analyses on these 52 economic development programs that are authorized to support entrepreneurs because these are the programs that appeared to overlap the most within the four agencies whose missions focus on economic development. We reviewed statutory and regulatory authority for each program on the activities and services the agencies can conduct to administer each of the programs. Because there was significant overlap and fragmentation among programs that provide technical assistance (for example, business training and counseling and support for research and development) to entrepreneurs (35 of the 52 programs), we focused on how the agencies provide this assistance. We reviewed agency documents and conducted interviews in both headquarters and the field to determine how technical assistance is provided to entrepreneurs and the extent of agency collaboration at the local level. We interviewed 14 officials from four federal agencies, 9 officials from two regional commissions, four entrepreneurs who have received federal support, and five state and local partners in select geographic areas where there was evidence of ongoing collaboration between the federal agencies. These geographic areas included both urban and rural areas. We assessed this technical assistance information against promising collaborative practices that we have previously identified.[4] For all 52 programs, we also evaluated the agencies' methods for tracking the activities conducted and assistance provided against standards for internal controls that we have previously identified.[5] For each program, we reviewed information on

---

[3]In a letter dated August 31, 2011, to the Comptroller General, the Chairwoman of the Senate Committee on Agriculture, Nutrition and Forestry asked, among other things, that we address a number of issues involving the potential for overlap, duplication, and fragmentation in economic development programs administered by the four agencies.

[4]GAO, *Results-Oriented Government: Practices That Can Help Enhance and Sustain Collaboration among Federal Agencies*, GAO-06-15 (Washington, D.C.: Oct. 21, 2005).

[5]GAO, *Standards for Internal Control in the Federal Government*, GAO/AIMD-00-21.3.1 (Washington, D.C.: Nov. 1, 1999).

program mission and goals, performance goals and accomplishments, and program evaluations conducted during the last decade. We evaluated this information against promising practices of leading organizations and the requirements of the GPRA Modernization Act of 2010. Appendix I provides more information on our scope and methodology.

We conducted this performance audit from June 2011 to July 2012 in accordance with generally accepted government auditing standards. Those standards require that we plan and perform the audit to obtain sufficient, appropriate evidence to provide a reasonable basis for our findings and conclusions based on our audit objectives. We believe that the evidence obtained provides a reasonable basis for our findings and conclusions based on our audit objectives.

Background

Fragmentation, Overlap, and Duplication

Fragmentation refers to circumstances in which more than one federal agency (or more than one organization within an agency) is involved in the same broad area of national interest. Overlap involves programs that have similar goals, devise similar strategies and activities to achieve those goals, or target similar users. Duplication occurs when two or more agencies or programs are engaged in the same activities or provide the same assistance to the same beneficiaries. In some instances, it may be appropriate for multiple agencies or entities to be involved in the same programmatic or policy area due to the nature or magnitude of the federal effort. However, we have previously identified instances where multiple government programs or activities have led to inefficiencies, and we determined that greater efficiencies or effectiveness might be achievable.[6]

---

[6]See GAO-12-342SP.

Defining Federal Economic Development Programs

In September 2000, we reported that there is no commonly accepted definition for economic development.[7] Absent a common definition, we subsequently developed a list of nine activities most often associated with economic development.[8] In general, we focused on economic activities that directly affected the overall development of an area, such as job creation, rather than on activities that improved individuals' quality of life, such as housing and education. The nine economic activities are

- supporting entrepreneurial efforts,

- supporting business incubators and accelerators,

- constructing and renovating commercial buildings,

- constructing and renovating industrial parks and buildings,

- strategic planning and research,

- marketing and access to new markets for products and industries,

- supporting telecommunications and broadband infrastructure,

- supporting physical infrastructure, and

- supporting tourism.

Appendix II provides illustrative examples of each of these economic activities. Appendix III provides more information on the 52 economic development programs we focused on for this report. Appendix IV includes a list of additional programs that are administered by federal agencies we identified that can fund at least one of these activities.

---

[7]See GAO, *Economic Development: Multiple Federal Programs Fund Similar Economic Development Activities*, GAO/RCED/GGD-00-220 (Washington, D.C.: Sept. 29, 2000).

[8]See GAO, *Rural Economic Development: More Assurance Is Needed That Grant Funding Information Is Accurately Reported*, GAO-06-294 (Washington, D.C.: Feb. 24, 2006).

GAO-12-819 Entrepreneurial Assistance

GPRA Modernization Act of 2010

In January 2011, Congress updated the Government Performance and Results Act of 1993 (GPRA) with the GPRA Modernization Act of 2010 (GPRAMA). GPRAMA establishes a new framework aimed at taking a more crosscutting and integrated approach to focusing on results and improving government performance. Effective implementation of GPRAMA could play an important role in clarifying desired outcomes; addressing program performance spanning multiple organizations; and facilitating future actions to reduce unnecessary duplication, overlap, and fragmentation. Among other things, GPRAMA requires the Office of Management and Budget (OMB) to coordinate with agencies to establish outcome-oriented federal government priority goals covering a limited number of policy areas, as well as goals to improve management across the federal government. It also requires OMB—in conjunction with the agencies—to develop a federal government performance plan that outlines how they will make progress toward achieving goals, including federal government priority goals. The President's 2013 budget submission includes the first interim federal government priority goals, including one to increase federal services to entrepreneurs and small businesses with an emphasis on start-ups and growing firms and underserved markets.[9]

Fragmented Programs Overlap, and Agencies' Efforts to Collaborate Have Been Limited

The identified economic development programs that support entrepreneurs overlap based on both the type of assistance they provide and the characteristics of the beneficiaries they target. This overlap among fragmented programs can make it difficult for entrepreneurs to navigate the services available to them. In addition, while agencies have taken steps to collaborate more in administering these programs, they have not implemented a number of good collaborative practices we have previously identified, and some entrepreneurs struggle to find the support they need.

---

[9]GAO, *Managing for Results: GAO's Work Related to the Interim Crosscutting Priority Goals under the GPRA Modernization Act*, GAO-12-620R (Washington, D.C.: May 12, 2012). We identified additional programs at Commerce, HUD, SBA, and USDA that can assist entrepreneurs with access to financing, mentorship and counseling services, and government contracts and research grants, and we recommended that the Director of OMB review the additional departments, agencies, and programs that we identified, and consider including them in the federal government's performance plan, as appropriate. OMB staff agreed with our recommendation that OMB review the additional departments, agencies, and programs that we have identified and determine if they are relevant to achieving the crosscutting goals.

Many Programs Are Authorized to Provide Similar Types of Assistance and Target Similar Beneficiaries

Federal efforts to support entrepreneurs are fragmented, which occurs when more than one agency or program is involved in the same broad area of national interest. Commerce (8), HUD (12), SBA (19), and USDA (13) administered 52 programs that could support entrepreneurial efforts in fiscal year 2011. Several types of overlap—which occurs when programs have similar goals, engage in similar activities or strategies to achieve them, or target similar beneficiaries—exist among these programs, based on the type of assistance the programs offer and characteristics of the programs' targeted beneficiaries.

Many of the programs provide entrepreneurs with similar types of assistance. The programs generally can be grouped according to at least one of three types of assistance that address different entrepreneurial needs: help obtaining (1) technical assistance, (2) financial assistance, and (3) government contracts. Many of the programs can provide more than one type of assistance, and most focus on technical assistance, financial assistance, or both:[10]

- *Technical assistance*: Thirty-five programs distributed across the four agencies can provide technical assistance, including business training, counseling and research, and development support.[11]

- *Financial assistance*: Thirty programs distributed across the four agencies can support entrepreneurs through financial assistance in the form of grants and loans.[12]

---

[10]SBA administers two programs that solely provide entrepreneurs with assistance in obtaining government contracts: the Historically Underutilized Business Zone (HUBZone) program, which supports small businesses located in economically distressed areas, and the Procurement Assistance to Small Businesses program, which serves small businesses located in any area.

[11]The number of programs administered by Commerce, HUD, SBA, and USDA that were identified in GAO-12-342SP as supporting technical assistance decreased from 36 to 35 because USDA's Empowerment Zones program is no longer active.

[12]The number of programs administered by Commerce, HUD, SBA, and USDA that were identified in GAO-12-342SP as supporting financial assistance decreased from 33 to 30 because USDA's Empowerment Zones program is no longer active and because subsequent to that report, Commerce told us that its Minority Business Centers and Native American Business Enterprise Centers programs only support technical assistance.

- *Government contracting assistance*: Five programs, all of which are administered by SBA, can support entrepreneurs by helping them qualify for federal procurement opportunities.[13]

We reviewed the statutes and regulations for each program and found that overlap tends to be concentrated among programs that provide a broad range of technical and financial assistance. Within the technical assistance category, 24 of the 35 programs are authorized to provide or fund a broad range of technical assistance both to entrepreneurs with existing businesses and to nascent entrepreneurs—that is, entrepreneurs attempting to start a business—in any industry. This broad range of support can include any form of training or counseling, including start-up assistance, access to capital, and accounting. Examples of programs in this category include Commerce's Minority Business Centers, five of HUD's Community Development Block Grant (CDBG) programs, SBA's Small Business Development Centers, and USDA's Rural Business Opportunity Grants.[14] Eight additional programs can support limited types of technical assistance or industries.[15] For example, Commerce's Trade Adjustment Assistance for Firms only supports existing businesses negatively affected by imports, and USDA's Small Socially-Disadvantaged Producer Grants only serves agricultural businesses.

Similarly, 16 of the 30 financial assistance programs can provide or guarantee loans that can be used for a broad range of purposes to existing businesses and nascent entrepreneurs in any industry. Examples of programs in this category include Commerce's Economic Adjustment Assistance programs, six of HUD's CDBG programs, SBA's 7(a) Loan Program, and USDA's Business and Industry Loans. Five other programs

---

[13]The number of programs administered by Commerce, HUD, SBA, and USDA that were identified in GAO-12-342SP as supporting government contracting assistance decreased from seven to five because subsequent to that report, Commerce told us that its Minority Business Centers and Native American Business Enterprise Centers programs only support technical assistance.

[14]Of the eight HUD CDBG programs, five operate in different areas of the United States that do not geographically overlap, one can only provide support to areas recovering from presidentially declared disasters, and two can operate in any area of the United States.

[15]The other three technical assistance programs are Commerce's Economic Development–Support for Planning Organizations, Economic Development–Technical Assistance, and Grants for Public Works and Economic Development Facilities, which support assistance to economic development organizations and local governments, which in turn support businesses.

GAO-12-819 Entrepreneurial Assistance

can support loans for a more narrow range of purposes or industries, while the other nine programs can only support other types of financial assistance, such as grants, equity investments, and surety guarantees.[16]

In addition, a number of programs overlap based on the characteristics of the targeted beneficiary. Most programs either target or exclusively serve one of four types of businesses: businesses in rural areas, businesses in economically distressed areas, disadvantaged businesses, and small businesses.[17] For example, all of HUD's 12 programs that can provide support to entrepreneurs are focused on serving beneficiaries in economically distressed areas or target benefits at low- to moderate-income individuals. SBA's 19 programs are all limited to serving small businesses, with several programs that either target or exclusively serve disadvantaged businesses and microenterprises.[18] Eight of USDA's 13 programs are limited to rural service areas, and four of these programs are limited to small businesses or microenterprises. Among Commerce's eight programs, six are limited to serving beneficiaries in economically distressed areas, while two exclusively serve disadvantaged businesses.

---

[16]Equity investments are capital provided to a business to purchase common or preferred stock, or a similar instrument. SBA can guarantee surety bonds (that is, an agreement between a surety company and the owner of a project that a contract will be completed) for contracts up to $2 million. These contracts can cover bonds for small and emerging contractors who cannot obtain surety bonds through regular commercial channels. SBA's guarantee gives sureties an incentive to provide bonding for eligible contractors and thereby strengthens a contractor's ability to obtain bonding and greater access to contracting opportunities.

[17]The definition of rural varies among these programs, but according to USDA—the agency that administers many of the economic development programs that serve rural areas—the term rural typically covers areas with population limits ranging from less than 2,500 to 50,000. Based on statutory language, we characterize economically distressed areas as communities with high concentrations of low- and moderate-income families or high rates of unemployment and/or underemployment. See, e.g., 42 U.S.C. § 3141; 42 U.S.C. § 5301. Likewise, based on statutory language, we characterize disadvantaged businesses as those owned by women, minority groups, and veterans, among other factors. See, e.g., 15 U.S.C. § 637(a); 15 U.S.C. § 656. The definition of small business varies among these programs, but according to SBA—the agency that administers many of the economic development programs that serve small businesses—the term small business refers to businesses that have annual receipts or total employee numbers under an agency-defined value for their specific industry.

[18]Microenterprises are generally defined as commercial enterprises that have ten or fewer employees.

Entrepreneurs may fall into more than one beneficiary category—for example, an entrepreneur may be in an area that is both rural and economically distressed. Therefore, these entrepreneurs would be eligible, based on program authority, for more than one subset of program. For example, a small business in a rural, economically distressed area, such as Susquehanna County, Pennsylvania, could, in terms of program authority, receive a broad range of technical assistance through at least nine programs at all four of the agencies, including:

- Commerce's Economic Adjustment Assistance;

- HUD's CDBG/States, Rural Innovation Fund, and Section 4 Capacity Building;

- SBA's SCORE and Small Business Development Centers;[19] and

- USDA's 1890 Land Grant Institutions, Rural Business Enterprise Grants, and Rural Business Opportunity Grants.[20]

Similarly, a small business that is both minority- and women-owned in an urban, noneconomically distressed area, such as Seattle, Washington, could in terms of program authority, receive a broad range of technical assistance through at least seven programs at three of the four agencies, including:

- Commerce's Minority Business Centers;

- HUD's CDBG/Entitlement and Section 4 Capacity Building; and

- SBA's Program for Investment in Micro-entrepreneurs (PRIME), SCORE, Small Business Development Centers, and Women's Business Centers.

---

[19]SCORE, formerly Service Corps of Retired Executives, provides technical assistance support for small business, start-ups and entrepreneurs.

[20]HUD's Rural Innovation Fund program did not receive funding in fiscal year 2011 but is still active. USDA's 1890 Land Grant Institutions received an unspecified amount of funding through USDA's Salaries and Expense account rather than program appropriations.

Entrepreneurs may also be eligible for multiple subsets of financial assistance programs based on their specific characteristics. For example, a small business in a rural, economically distressed area, such as Bourbon County, Kansas, could in terms of authority, receive financial assistance in the form of guaranteed or direct loans for a broad range of uses through at least eight programs at the four agencies, including:

- Commerce's Economic Adjustment Assistance;

- HUD's CDBG/States, Rural Innovation Fund and Section 4 Capacity Building;

- SBA's 7(a) Loan Program and Small Business Investment Companies; and

- USDA's Business and Industry Loans and Rural Business Enterprise Grants.

A small business that is both minority and women-owned in an urban, noneconomically distressed area, such as Raleigh, North Carolina, could receive financial assistance in the form of guaranteed or direct loans for a broad range of uses through at least four programs at two of the four agencies, including:

- HUD's CDBG/Entitlement and Section 4 Capacity Building; and

- SBA's 7(a) Loan Program and Small Business Investment Companies.

Five programs provide government contracting assistance to entrepreneurs, but our analysis did not identify significant overlap in the types of assistance these programs provide or the types of entrepreneurs they serve. While these five programs are all administered by SBA and can serve businesses in any industry, they tend to target specific types of entrepreneurs and provide unique types of assistance. For example, the Procurement Assistance to Small Businesses program coordinates access to government contracts for small and disadvantaged businesses with other federal agencies, while the 8(a) Business Development Program coordinates certification of eligible disadvantaged businesses for the contracts made available at these other agencies, in addition to providing business development assistance during their 9-year term.[21]

While many programs overlap in terms of statutory authority, entrepreneurs may in reality have fewer options to access assistance from multiple programs. Agencies often rely on intermediaries (that is, third-party entities such as nonprofit organizations, higher education institutions, or local governments that use federal grants to provide eligible assistance directly to entrepreneurs) to provide specific support to entrepreneurs, and these intermediaries vary in terms of their location and the types of assistance they provide. For example, while entrepreneurs seeking technical assistance in Susquehanna County, Pennsylvania, are eligible to receive this support through USDA's 1890 Land Grant Institutions program, the closest funded intermediary is in Delaware, making it unlikely that such an entrepreneur would utilize services through this program. Additionally, intermediaries we spoke to in several areas said they typically provide a more limited range of services to entrepreneurs than are allowed under their statutory authority. For example, two intermediaries that we interviewed in Texas that were authorized to provide a broad range of technical support to entrepreneurs through SBA's Small Business Development Center and Commerce's Minority Business Center noted that they each specialized in a narrower subset of services and referred beneficiaries to each other and other resources for some services outside of their niches. Specifically, the intermediary at the Small Business Development Center noted that they provide a range of long-term services to small businesses over different phases of development, while the intermediary at the Minority Business Center noted that they focused specifically on larger minority-owned firms as well as start-up companies.

Overlapping programs may also employ different mechanisms to provide similar types of support to entrepreneurs. For example, programs may support technical assistance through different types of intermediaries that provide services to entrepreneurs. USDA's Rural Business Opportunity Grants program can provide technical assistance through local governments, nonprofit corporations, Indian tribes, and cooperatives that are located in rural areas, while SBA's SCORE program utilizes retired

---

[21]SBA's 8(a) program, named for a section of the Small Business Act, is a development program created to help small, disadvantaged businesses compete in the American economy and access the federal procurement market.

GAO-12-819 Entrepreneurial Assistance

business professionals and others that volunteer their time to provide assistance. Additionally, programs may support financial assistance in the form of loans through loan guarantees, direct loans, or support for revolving loan funds. SBA's 7(a) Loan program provides guarantees on loans made by private sector lenders, while USDA's Intermediary Re-lending program provides financing to intermediaries to operate revolving loan funds.

Additionally, some programs distribute funding through multiple layers of intermediaries before it reaches entrepreneurs. For example, HUD's Section 4 Capacity Building program is only authorized to provide grants to five national organizations, which pass funding on to a number of local grantees, including community development corporations that may use the funding to provide technical or financial assistance to entrepreneurs. HUD officials also noted that most of their programs allow local grantees discretion on whether to use funds to support entrepreneurs or for other authorized purposes. Other programs may competitively award grants to multiple intermediaries working jointly in the same community to serve entrepreneurs. For example, Commerce's Economic Adjustment Assistance program can provide grants to intermediaries, such as consortiums of local governments and nonprofits, which in turn provide technical or financial assistance to entrepreneurs.

Although we identified a number of examples of statutory overlap, we did not find evidence of duplication among these programs (that is, instances when two or more agencies or programs are engaged in the same activities to provide the same services to the same beneficiaries) based on available data. However, most agencies were not able to provide the programmatic information, such as data on users of the program that is necessary to determine whether or not duplication actually exists among the programs. The agencies' data-collecting practices will be discussed at greater length later in this report.

Some Entrepreneurs Struggle to Navigate Technical Assistance Programs

As previously discussed, 35 programs distributed across the four agencies provide technical assistance, including business training and counseling. While the existence of multiple programs in and of itself is not a problem, the delivery system of these fragmented and overlapping technical assistance programs contains many components (see fig. 1). Several entrepreneurs and various technical assistance providers with whom we spoke—including agency field offices, intermediaries, and other local service providers—told us that the system can be confusing and that some entrepreneurs do not know what services are available or where to go for assistance. As discussed earlier, federal funds typically flow from the federal agencies to different eligible intermediaries, which are third-party entities that receive federal funds, such as nonprofits or universities. These intermediaries in turn may provide technical assistance to entrepreneurs by, for example, helping them to develop a business plan or put together a loan package to obtain financing. For instance, SBA's Women's Business Center and Commerce's Minority Business Center programs can provide technical assistance through different intermediaries, such as the Arkansas Women's Business Center and the University of Hawaii. Although intermediaries are the primary providers of technical assistance, agency field offices may also provide some technical assistance. For example, USDA's Rural Development state offices may provide advice on how to complete their respective grant applications. SBA's district offices may also discuss the different business structures available.

Figure 1: Fragmented Delivery System of Federally Funded Technical Assistance to Entrepreneurs

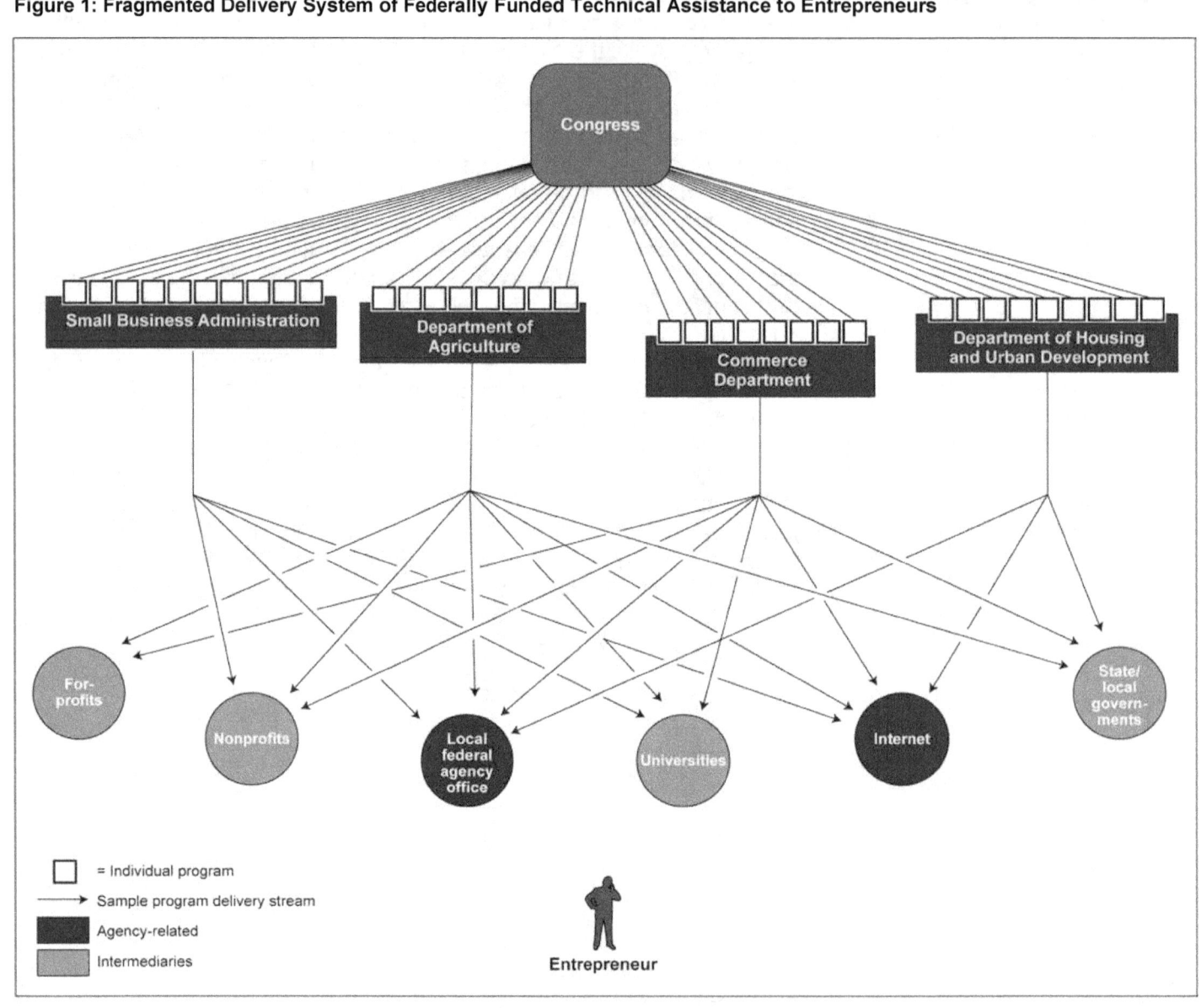

Source: GAO.

Note: While our work focuses on the four federal agencies' economic development programs that support entrepreneurs, many state governments also have economic development departments that assist, plan, and support economic development activities. Local governments and nonprofit organizations may also offer programs that can be used to support economic development activities. In addition, there may be other federal agencies involved with supporting economic development. Some intermediaries receive support from multiple public- and private-sector institutions, and some entrepreneurs we spoke with indicated that they had received assistance from multiple sources.

GAO-12-819 Entrepreneurial Assistance

Technical assistance providers sometimes attempt to help entrepreneurs navigate the system by referring them to other programs, but these efforts are not consistently successful. Some of these providers told us that they assess the entrepreneur's needs to determine whether to assist them or refer them to another entity that could provide the assistance more effectively. For example, if an 1890 Land Grant intermediary were not able to assist an entrepreneur, it might refer the entrepreneur to SBA, USDA, or a local provider. However, such referrals are not always successful. For example, an entrepreneur we spoke with described a case in which he needed assistance with developing a business plan but was unable to receive this assistance, even after several referrals. Some technical assistance providers that we spoke with either did not appear to fully understand other technical assistance programs or thought that others did not fully understand their programs. For example, one technical assistance provider told us that some technical assistance providers were focused on more established businesses, but when we reached out to some of these providers, they said they served all entrepreneurs. This lack of understanding could prevent providers from making helpful referrals and leveraging other programs and limit the effectiveness of the programs.

In addition, programs' Internet resources can also be difficult to navigate. Each agency has its own separate website that provides information to entrepreneurs, but they often direct entrepreneurs to other websites for additional information. For example, the SBA website directs users to another website that lists the Small Business Development Centers, which then directs users to another website that provides some information on the centers' available services. SBA, Commerce, USDA, and other agencies have recently collaborated to develop a joint website called BusinessUSA with the goal of making it easier for businesses to access services. However, the site was not fully operational as of June 2012, and none of the entrepreneurs and almost all the technical assistance providers we spoke with were not yet aware of it. As of June 2012, this website listed a number of potential technical assistance programs across different federal agencies with links to the programs' websites. Some technical assistance providers and entrepreneurs suggested that a single source to help entrepreneurs quickly find information instead of sorting through different websites would be helpful.

Agencies' Collaboration Has Been Limited

Enhanced collaboration between agencies could potentially address some of the difficulties entrepreneurs experience and improve program efficiency. In prior work we identified practices that can help to enhance and sustain collaboration among federal agencies, which can help to maximize performance and results, and have recommended that the agencies follow them.[22] These collaborative practices include identifying common outcomes, establishing joint strategies, leveraging resources, determining roles and responsibilities, and developing compatible policies and procedures. In addition, GPRAMA requires agencies to describe in annual performance plans how they are working with other agencies to achieve their performance goals and relevant federal government performance goals.[23]

The agencies have taken initial steps to improve how they collaborate to provide technical assistance to entrepreneurs by, for example, entering into formal agreements with each other, but they have not pursued a number of other good collaborative practices we have previously identified, as the following examples illustrate:

- USDA and SBA entered into a formal agreement in April 2010 to coordinate their efforts aimed at supporting businesses in rural areas. In April 2011, USDA began to survey its state offices to help the agency gauge the level of collaboration between its field staff and SBA, as well as to identify additional opportunities to enhance collaboration. However, the agencies' business development programs that can support start-up businesses—USDA's Rural Business Enterprise Grant and SBA's Small Business Development Centers—have yet to determine roles and responsibilities, find ways to leverage each other's resources, or establish compatible policies and procedures to collaboratively support rural businesses.

- The Appalachian Regional Development Initiative is a formal agreement, which began in November 2010, among the Appalachian Regional Commission (which coordinates economic development activities in the Appalachian region), the four agencies, and other

---

[22]GAO-06-15.

[23]Pub. L. No. 111-352, 124 Stat. 3866 (2011).

agencies.[24] This agreement is intended to strengthen and diversify the Appalachian economy through better deployment and coordination of federal resources. According to officials at the Appalachian Regional Commission, the agencies did participate in a joint workshop to present the locally available resources from business development to infrastructure in the fall 2011, and USDA is one of its stronger partners. However, the agencies have not established joint strategies, determined roles and responsibilities, or developed compatible policies and procedures for carrying out the common outcomes outlined in their agreements at the local level where technical assistance is provided.

- In August 2011 SBA and the Delta Regional Authority (which coordinates economic development activities in the Delta region) entered into a formal agreement to better deploy and coordinate resources for small businesses located in the Delta region.[25] As part of this agreement, in April 2012 the two entities announced a joint effort to launch an program to support entrepreneurs called Operation JumpStart. Operation JumpStart is designed as a hands-on, microenterprise development program that is intended to help entrepreneurs test the feasibility of their business ideas and plan to launch new ventures. However, their effort thus far has been limited. While they entered into a formal agreement to launch the program, this agreement did not include any determinations of specific roles and responsibilities or establish compatible policies and procedures to collaboratively support these small businesses.

- In June 2011, the President created the White House Rural Council to promote economic prosperity in rural areas. It is chaired by the Secretary of Agriculture and includes HUD, Commerce, SBA, and other agencies. The council is working to better coordinate federal programs in order to maximize the impact of federal investment in rural areas. Even though the council has announced a number of initiatives, such as helping rural small businesses access capital, the

---

[24]The Appalachian region is made up of 420 counties in parts of 12 states—Alabama, Georgia, Kentucky, Maryland, Mississippi, New York, North Carolina, Ohio, Pennsylvania, South Carolina, Tennessee, and Virginia—as well as all of West Virginia.

[25]The Delta region is made up of 252 counties and parishes in parts of eight states— Alabama, Arkansas, Illinois, Kentucky, Louisiana, Mississippi, Missouri, and Tennessee.

agencies have yet to implement many of our other good collaborative practices.

In addition, while most of these agencies at the headquarters level have agreed to work together by signing formal agreements to administer some of their similar programs, the agencies generally have yet to develop compatible guidance to implement these agreements in the field. As noted previously, some intermediaries we spoke with that provide technical assistance through agency programs collaborate by referring entrepreneurs to other federal programs and agencies that they believe may better meet their needs. However these efforts are inconsistent and do not always result in entrepreneurs obtaining the services they are seeking. OMB and the four agencies also have recently taken steps to implement GPRAMA, which requires them to coordinate better; however, implementation was still in the early phases as of May 2012 and had not yet affected how they administer their programs.

Implementing additional good collaborative practices could improve how the federal government supports entrepreneurs by, for example, helping agencies make more useful referrals, meet more diverse needs of entrepreneurs, and present a more consistent delivery system to entrepreneurs:

- Collaborating agencies that agree upon roles and responsibilities can clarify who will do what, organize their joint and individual efforts, and facilitate coordinated decision making. This effort could help agencies not only initiate and sustain collaboration but also determine who is in the best position to support an entrepreneur based on the client's need, which could lead to more effective referrals.

- Because collaborating agencies bring different resources and capacities to their efforts, they can look for opportunities to leverage each other's resources, thus obtaining additional benefits that would not be available if they were working separately. Being able to leverage each other's resources could help agencies more effectively and efficiently support entrepreneurs because they may be able to meet more diverse needs by drawing on one another's strengths.

- Compatible standards, policies, procedures, and data systems could help to sustain collaborative efforts. As agencies standardize, for example, procedures for supporting entrepreneurs, they can more efficiently support entrepreneurs through more consistent service-delivery methods across agencies and programs. This could be particularly helpful for entrepreneurs who are not familiar with the federal programs.

In addition, GPRAMA's crosscutting framework requires that agencies collaborate in order to address issues such as economic development that transcend more than one agency, and GPRAMA directs agencies to describe how they are working with each other to achieve their program goals. As discussed previously, without more substantial collaboration, the delivery of service to entrepreneurs, particularly those who are unfamiliar with federal economic development programs, may not be as effective and efficient as possible.

Agencies Lack Information to Track Program Activities and Measure Performance

Agencies do not maintain information in a way that would enable them to track activities for most of their programs. Further, the agencies lack information on why some programs have failed to meet some or all of their goals. While information from program evaluations can help measure program effectiveness, agencies have conducted evaluations of only 20 of the 52 active programs since 2000.

Agencies Do Not Maintain Information to Enable Tracking of Activities for Most Programs

While the four agencies collected at least some information on program activities in either an electronic records system or through paper files, most were unable to summarize the information in a way that could be used to help administer the programs. Promising practices of program administration that we have identified include a strong capacity to collect and analyze accurate, useful, and timely data.[26] According to OMB, being able to track and measure specific program data can help agencies diagnose problems, identify drivers of future performance, evaluate risk, support collaboration, and inform follow-up actions. Analyses of patterns

---

[26]Harold I. Steinberg, *Using Performance Information to Drive Performance Improvement*, Association of Government Accountants CPAG Research Series: Report No. 29 (Alexandria, VA: Dec. 2011).

and anomalies can also help agencies discover ways to achieve more value for the taxpayer's money. In addition, agencies can use this information to assess whether their specific program activities are contributing as planned to the agency goals.

In addition, government internal control standards state that agencies should promptly and accurately record transactions to maintain their relevance and value for management decision making. Furthermore, this information should be readily available for use by management and others so that they can carry out their duties with the goal of achieving all of their objectives, including making operating decisions and allocating resources.[27] This guidance calls for agencies to go beyond merely collecting information, stating that they should systematically analyze, or track, it over time to inform decision making. For example, the agencies could track this information to identify trends on how the programs are being used in different areas of the country. This information could help the agencies strategically target program resources to support the unique needs in each geographic area.

All four agencies collect program information but do not track detailed, readily available information for most programs, such as the type of technical assistance that their programs provide or fund, which is necessary to effectively administer their programs. For example, Commerce's Economic Adjustment Assistance, HUD's Section 4 Capacity Building, SBA's PRIME, and USDA's Rural Business Opportunity Grant Program can all support a broad range of technical assistance to various types of entrepreneurs, but agencies are unable to provide information on the types of services provided that would be necessary to compare activities across programs. Similarly, the agencies typically do not track detailed information on the characteristics of entrepreneurs that they serve, such as whether they are located in rural or economically distressed areas or the entrepreneurs' type of industry. Most of the agencies collect detailed information on several of their programs in a way that could potentially help them more efficiently administer their programs, as the following examples illustrate:

---

[27]GAO/AIMD-00-21.3.1.

- SBA collects detailed information on the type of technical assistance provided and type of entrepreneur served for 5 of its 10 technical assistance programs. SBA categorizes the types of technical assistance it provides by 17 categories of training and counseling, such as helping a business develop its business plan. All of this information is maintained in an electronic database that is accessible by agency staff.

- For all of its programs, USDA collects detailed information on the industry of each of the entrepreneurs it supports. In addition, USDA collects detailed information (19 categories) on how entrepreneurs use proceeds, such as for working capital, provided through five of its financial assistance programs. USDA maintains this information in an electronic database, and officials stated that they can provide this type of detailed information upon request.

- For all eight of its technical assistance programs, Commerce collects information on the type of entrepreneur served and the entrepreneurs' industry.

While HUD tracked limited program information on the type of support it provides to entrepreneurs, the agency collects information on other program activities and uses it to monitor program compliance. HUD staff meet quarterly with the Secretary of HUD to discuss these program data and determine changes that should be made to improve how they carry out program activities. Table 1 summarizes the type of information that agencies maintain in a readily available format that could be tracked to help administer the programs.

Table 1: Programs that Can Support Entrepreneurs and Maintain Readily Available Information, by Agency

		35 technical assistance programs				
		Commerce (8)	HUD (9)	SBA (10)	USDA (8)	Total (35)
Type of technical assistance provided?	yes	2	0	5	0	7
	no	6	9	5	8	28
Industry entrepreneur is working in?	yes	8	0	5	8	21
	no	0	9	5	0	14
Type of entrepreneur by targeted categories?[a]	yes	8	1	5	7	21
	no	0	8	5	1	14
		30 financial assistance programs				
		Commerce (2)	HUD (10)	SBA (10)	USDA (8)	Total (30)
Type of financial assistance provided?	yes	2	8	9	8	27
	no	0	2	1	0	3
Use of proceeds?	yes	2	1	7	5	15
	no	0	9	3	3	15
Industry entrepreneur is working in?	yes	2	0	5	8	15
	no	0	10	5	0	15
Type of entrepreneur by targeted categories?	yes	2	3	8	5	18
	no	0	7	2	3	12

Source: GAO analysis of information provided by Commerce, HUD, USDA, and SBA.

Note: This table is based on 50 of the 52 programs that can support entrepreneurs because we excluded the 2 SBA programs that only support government contracting assistance. Some of the 50 programs can provide both financial and technical assistance.

[a]Targeted categories can include businesses in rural or economically distressed areas, disadvantaged businesses, or small businesses.

Officials who administer these programs provided a number of reasons why they do not track detailed program information for all programs in a way that could be used for program administration purposes. For example, some officials stated they do not rely on program information with this level of detail to make decisions about their programs. As previously discussed, many of these programs are administered by intermediaries, and these intermediaries may maintain detailed information on the services they provide. Agencies do not always require the intermediaries to forward all of this detailed information to headquarters. Rather, an intermediary may, for example, submit data summaries of the support they have provided during the reporting period in a narrative format—a format that cannot be easily aggregated or analyzed. Other agency officials noted that this type of summary-level information they collect and maintain at headquarters is sufficient for their purposes and complies with OMB reporting guidelines. However, without tracking more detailed program information, such as the specific type of support provided and the entrepreneurs served, agencies may not be able to make informed decisions or identify risks and problem areas within their programs based on factors such as how entrepreneurs make use of program services or funding. Furthermore, agencies may not be able to understand the extent that their programs are serving their intended purposes.

Some Programs Failed to Meet Their Goals

Our review found that for fiscal year 2011, a number of programs that support entrepreneurs failed to meet some or all of their performance goals. Measuring performance allows organizations to track the progress they are making toward their goals and gives managers crucial information on which to base their organizational and management decisions. Leading organizations recognize that performance measures can create powerful incentives to influence organizational and individual behavior. Some of their good practices include setting and measuring performance goals. GPRAMA requires agencies to develop annual performance plans that include performance goals for an agency's program activities and accompanying performance measures. According to GPRAMA, these performance goals should be in a quantifiable and measurable form to define the level of performance to be achieved for program activities each year. The agencies should also be able to identify which external factors might affect goal accomplishment and explain why a goal was not met. Such plans can help to reinforce the connection between the long-term strategic goals outlined in their strategic plans and the day-to-day activities of their managers and staff.

We found that of the 33 programs that support entrepreneurs and set goals, 19 did not meet any of their goals or only met some of their goals (see table 2).[28] These programs include Commerce's Economic Development/Support for Planning Organizations, HUD's Indian Community Development Block Grant, SBA's 504 loan, and USDA's Rural Business Opportunity Grant programs. Appendix III provides more information on fiscal year 2011 goals and accomplishments for each program that has goals and accomplishment data available.

Table 2: Accomplishment Data for 33 Programs that Support Entrepreneurs and Set Goals, Fiscal Year 2011

	Programs that did not meet goals	Programs that met some goals	Programs that met all goals
Commerce	1	5	2
HUD	2	0	0
SBA	2	5	7
USDA	4	0	3
Total	**9**	**10**	**12**

Source: GAO analysis of data from Commerce, HUD, SBA, and USDA.

Note: Two programs have goals but did not have goal accomplishment information. Goal accomplishment information for HUD's Section 4 Capacity Building for Affordable Housing and Community Development program is unknown because HUD did not provide goal accomplishment information. Goal accomplishment information for USDA's Small Business Innovation Research program is not available because the program goals are based on 2-year time periods and the current period has not yet ended.

Agency officials provided a number of reasons why they thought these programs did not meet their goals, including that the goals were estimates and program funding was lower than anticipated. In addition, some agency officials could not identify any causes for the failure to meet goals nor had they attempted to determine the specific reasons for the failures.

---

[28]Nineteen programs did not have fiscal year 2011 performance goals: HUD's CDBG Insular Areas, CDBG Entitlement, CDBG States, CDBG Non-entitlement Grants in Hawaii, Section 108, CDBG Disaster Recovery, Rural Innovation Fund, Hispanic Serving Institutions Assisting Communities, and Alaska Native/Native Hawaiian Institutions Assisting Communities; SBA's PRIME, Small Business Innovation Research, Small Business Technology Transfer, New Markets Venture Capital, and Federal and State Technology Partnership programs; and USDA's Small Socially-Disadvantaged Producer Grants, 1890's Land Grants Institutions, Agriculture Innovation Center, Biomass Research and Development Initiative, and Woody Biomass Utilization Grants. While the agencies are not required to have goals for each program, agency officials said that 6 of the 19 programs did not have goals because they were either temporary, were not funded, or were marked for elimination by agencies. One of the 19 programs that did not meet its goals was not funded in fiscal year 2011.

Programs that are failing to meet performance goals without a clear understanding of the reasons could result in agencies not being able to identify and address specific parts of programs that may not be working well. Additionally, without more detailed data on the activities of individual intermediaries, determining which of these third-parties are effectively administering these programs and helping meet program goals is difficult. Making decisions without this information could result in scarce resources being directed away from programs, or intermediaries, that are effective and towards those that are not meeting their objectives or struggling to meet their objectives.

Agencies Have Not Evaluated the Majority of Programs That Support Entrepreneurs

Over the past 12 years, agencies have conducted program evaluations of 20 of the 52 programs that support entrepreneurs.[29] Most of these 20 programs were evaluated once in the past decade. The studies that were conducted focus on a variety of areas, including customer satisfaction and the programs' economic impacts, and report an array of findings related to the effectiveness of the programs. For example, some evaluations reported the actual number of jobs produced as a result of program investments, while one evaluation reported that programs were more useful for larger firms than smaller firms. Some of the differences among the findings are tied to the varying questions the studies sought to answer and the methods that were used to answer them. The questions and methods employed are typically informed by the organization's purpose for pursuing these studies. These purposes could include, for example, assessing program impact, identifying areas for improvement, or guiding resource allocation. Figure 2 describes the scope of each program evaluation and the findings related to program effectiveness. Appendix V provides more information on each program evaluation.

---

[29]We reviewed the methodologies of these studies to ensure they were sound and determined they were sufficiently reliable to report high-level findings related to the programs' overall effectiveness.

GAO-12-819 Entrepreneurial Assistance

Figure 2: Evaluations of Programs that Support Entrepreneurs, 2000-2012

Agency	Program (year review completed)	Selected findings related to program effectiveness
Commerce	Grants for Public Works and Economic Development Facilities (2008)	EDA investments were associated with an increase in jobs.
	Economic Adjustment Assistance (2005, 2008)	For rural areas, the type of project is an important determinant of the number of jobs created. Business incubators are the most effective projects, while roads projects are the least effective.
	Economic Development/Technical Assistance (2001, 2003)	The program serves as a facilitator or as an impetus to stimulate economic development in targeted areas. For example, it helps to obtain stakeholder buy-in and ignition of the process. The program does not achieve, by itself, the ultimate goal of job creation or increase in income. However, the program (1) lacks oversight and accountability mechanisms to encourage higher and more uniform performance levels; (2) there is no systematic follow-up survey to measure the longer-term economic impacts of assistance; and (3) EDA regional offices often lack adequate oversight staff.
	Economic Development/ Support for Planning Organizations (2002)	Projects do not meet their goals.
HUD	CDBG/Entitlement Grants (2002, 2002)	There are links between larger CDBG investments and improvements in neighborhood quality, such as increases in business and employment. The survival rate for start-ups that received benefits from CDBG or Section 108 had a better survival rate than 50% of U.S. start-ups in general. More than 50% of CDBG- and Section 108-assisted projects met or exceeded their total job creation and retention targets.
	CDBG/States (2002)	The survival rate for start-ups that received benefits from CDBG or Section 108 had a better survival rate than 50% of U.S. start-ups in general. More than 50% of CDBG- and Section 108-assisted projects met or exceeded their total job creation and retention targets.
	CDBG/Section 108 (2002)	
	CDBG/Brownfields Economic Development Initiative (2002)	
	CDBG/Indian (2006)	A significant portion (25 percent) of Indian CDBG projects had a positive effect on the quality of life for Native American and Alaska native communities. Grantees were able to leverage grants to obtain additional funds.
	Section 4 Capacity Building for Affordable Housing and Community Development (2011)	Community Development Corporations (CDC) reported that the program helped them increase their organization capacity (e.g., increase in number of staff). Also, the ones that received more grants implemented more activities. CDCs have developed almost 17 million square feet of commercial space between 2001 and 2009, compared with 2.7 million before 2001.
SBA	Small Business Development Centers (2010)	Larger firms indicated a greater degree of usefulness than smaller firms.
	Women's Business Centers (WBC) (2004, 2005, 2010)	Larger firms indicated a greater degree of usefulness than smaller firms. Clients served by WBCs saw an increase in profits, receipts, new jobs, and start-ups.
	SCORE (2010)	Larger firms indicated a greater degree of usefulness than smaller firms.
	7(a) Loan Program (2008, 2008)	Businesses saw an increase in sales and employment. Start-up and minority-owned businesses had the largest gains.
	504 Loan Program (2008, 2008)	
	Small Business Investment Company Program (SBIC) (2008, 2008)	Businesses saw an increase in sales and employment from 1999 to 2001, with start-up and minority-owned businesses having the largest gains. Businesses that participated in the SBIC program saw the largest gains and had the longest range of survival.
	Microloan Program (2008)	
	HUBZone (2008)	There are 2450 HUBZone areas and because the contract monies are spread so thin the program has no detectable impact on most zones and almost none on a national scale.
	Small Business Innovation Research Program (2008)	Technological innovation was achieved—an average of 1.66 scientific publication for each project, as well as networking with universities. Participation by minorities and women lagged other groups.
USDA	Value Added Producer Grants (2007)	

Program evaluation did not address the extent to which the program was achieving its mission

Source: GAO analysis of information provided by Commerce, HUD, SBA, and USDA.

Although GPRAMA does not require agencies to conduct formal program evaluations, it does require agencies to describe program evaluations that were used to establish or revise strategic goals as well as program evaluations they plan to conduct in the future. Additionally, while not required, agencies can use periodic program evaluations to complement ongoing performance measurement. Program evaluations that systematically study the benefits of programs may help identify the extent to which overlapping and fragmented programs are achieving their objectives. In addition, program evaluations can help agencies determine reasons why a performance goal was not met and give an agency direction on how to improve program performance. For instance, 8 of the 33 programs that were not evaluated by the administering agency failed to meet all of their performance goals. Performance evaluations could have helped agencies understand why these programs' goals were not met. Further, program evaluations, which examine a broader range of information than is feasible on an ongoing basis through performance measures, can help assess the impact and effectiveness of a program.[30]

While many of the agencies agree that performance evaluations can add value, some stated that they have limited funds and cannot afford performance evaluation studies. Other agency officials stated that they are not allowed to use program funds for evaluation. For example, USDA officials stated that they are not allowed to use program funds to study the effectiveness of the Small Business Innovation Research program. While program evaluations can be expensive, there are various methods that agencies can employ to make them more cost-effective. For example, agencies could conduct a program evaluation that relies on their own data to prevent them from purchasing data from a vendor.[31] Without periodic program evaluations, the agencies' ability to manage programs effectively and efficiently may be limited. Program evaluations can also potentially help agencies understand why some programs have failed to meet some or all of their goals, as previously discussed. Moreover, without this type

---

[30]GAO, *Program Evaluation: Studies Helped Agencies Measure or Explain Program Performance,* GAO/GGD-00-204 (Washington, D.C.: Sept. 29, 2000).

[31]In July 2007, we recommended that SBA further utilize the loan performance information it already collects to better report how small businesses fare after they participate in the 7(a) program. While SBA agreed with the recommendation, the agency has not implemented it. See GAO, *Small Business Administration: Additional Measures Needed to Assess 7(a) Loan Program's Performance,* GAO-07-769 (Washington, D.C.: Jul. 13, 2007).

GAO-12-819 Entrepreneurial Assistance

of information, Congress and the agencies may not be able to better ensure that scarce resources are being directed to the most effective programs and activities.

Conclusions

In order to support entrepreneurs, federal economic development programs must be efficient and accessible to the people they are intended to serve. However, navigating these overlapping and fragmented programs can be an ongoing challenge for some entrepreneurs. While the agencies have a number of interagency agreements in place, our review found that agency field staff do not consistently collaborate and may not be able to help entrepreneurs navigate the large number of programs available to them. We have identified practices that can help to support collaboration among federal agencies and programs. In addition, greater collaboration is one way agencies can help overcome overlap and fragmentation among programs within and across agencies. Moreover, without enhanced collaboration and coordination, agencies may not be able to make the best use of limited federal resources and may not reach their intended beneficiaries in the most effective and efficient manner.

In addition, given the number of federal programs focused on supporting entrepreneurs, agencies need specific information about these programs to best allocate limited federal resources and make decisions about better administering and structuring the programs. In our February 2012 report on duplication, overlap, and fragmentation, we expected to recommend that Congress tie funding to program performance and that OMB and the agencies explore opportunities to restructure programs through such means as consolidation or elimination. However, decisions about funding and restructuring would be difficult without better performance and evaluation information. Thus, making these recommendations would be premature until the agencies address a number of deficiencies. Specifically, agencies typically do not collect information that would enable them to track the services they provide and to whom they provide those services. This practice is not consistent with government standards for internal controls. Without such information, the agencies may not be able to administer the programs in a way that will result in the most efficient and effective federal support to entrepreneurs.

Moreover, most of the programs that set goals did not meet them or only met some of them, and agency officials could not always identify reasons why program goals were not met. Additionally, many of these programs have not been evaluated in 10 years or more. GPRAMA requires agencies to set and measure annual performance goals, and recognizes the value of program evaluations because they can help agencies assess programs' effectiveness and improve program performance. Agencies' lack of understanding of why programs have failed to meet goals may limit decision makers' ability to understand which programs are most effective and allocate federal resources accordingly.

Recommendations

To help improve the efficiency and effectiveness of federal efforts to support entrepreneurs, we make the following recommendations:

- The Director of the Office and Management and Budget, the Secretaries of the Departments of Agriculture, Commerce, and Housing and Urban Development, and the Administrator of the Small Business Administration should work together to identify opportunities to enhance collaboration among programs, both within and across agencies.

- The Secretaries of the Departments of Agriculture, Commerce, and Housing and Urban Development, and the Administrator of the Small Business Administration should consistently collect information that would enable them to track the specific type of assistance programs provide and the entrepreneurs they serve and use this information to help administer their programs.

- The Secretaries of the Departments of Agriculture, Commerce, and Housing and Urban Development, and the Administrator of the Small Business Administration should conduct more program evaluations to better understand why programs have not met performance goals and their overall effectiveness.

Agency Comments and Our Evaluation

GAO provided a draft of this report to OMB, Commerce, HUD, SBA, and USDA for review and comment. We also provided excerpts of appendix IV to all of the agencies with programs listed for their review. Commerce, HUD, and USDA provided written comments. Commerce, HUD, and SBA also provided technical comments, which were incorporated where appropriate. OMB did not provide comments on the draft report. All written comments are reprinted in appendixes VI, VII and VIII.

The Acting Secretary of Commerce stated that we may wish to consider the complementary role many agencies play in the field of economic development and the need for varied but complementary activities to address the complexities of entrepreneurs. She commented that what may appear as duplication at a higher level is in reality a portfolio of distinct services meeting unique needs. Our report notes that in some instances it may be appropriate for multiple agencies or entities to be involved in the same programmatic or policy area due to the nature or magnitude of the federal effort. We found that many of the 52 programs we examined overlap in terms of statutory authority; our report does not state that duplication exists among these programs. However, we found that most of these agencies were not able to provide programmatic information, such as data on users of the programs that is necessary to determine whether or not duplication actually exists.

The Acting Secretary also stated that federal agencies do successfully collaborate and forge policy partnerships, and noted that EDA plays a key role in leading and shaping federal policy for fostering collaborative regional economic development. As noted in our report, Commerce, HUD, SBA, and USDA have taken initial steps to improve how they collaborate to provide technical assistance to entrepreneurs and cites specific examples of these collaborative efforts. However, GAO found that the four agencies, including Commerce, have not pursued a number of other good collaborative practices we have previously identified. For example, our report states that the White House Rural Council, comprised of Commerce and other federal agencies, is working to better coordinate federal programs in order to maximize the impact of federal investment in rural areas. Although the council has announced a number of initiatives, such as helping rural small businesses access capital, we found that the agencies have yet to implement many of our other good collaborative practices such as developing compatible guidance to implement inter-agency agreements. For example, we found that while most of these agencies at the headquarters level have agreed to work together by signing formal agreements to administer some of their similar programs, the agencies generally have yet to develop compatible guidance to implement these agreements in the field.

Finally, the Acting Secretary stated that EDA agrees with our report's focus on the need for more specific information tracking and more frequent performance evaluation. She noted that EDA has established performance measures for each of its programs, and that these performance measures were subject to thorough review and validation procedures. She also noted that EDA routinely conducts evaluations of its programs (often limited only by lack of resources). However, the Acting Secretary stated that efforts to monitor and track project progress seem to have been outside of the scope of our report, based on many of the general statements made in the report about the need for additional work in this area. As previously stated, we found that most of the agencies were not able to provide programmatic information for programs that can support entrepreneurs. Our report also states that Commerce does collect information on the type of entrepreneur served and the entrepreneur's industry for all eight of its programs that can provide technical assistance; however, the report notes that Commerce does not collect information on the specific type of technical assistance provided to entrepreneurs for six of these eight programs—information necessary to compare activities across programs. We provided summary information on evaluations conducted by the agencies in the report, including Commerce. We also found that Commerce, HUD, SBA, and USDA had not evaluated the majority of the 52 programs that can support entrepreneurs, including four of the eight programs Commerce administers. We concluded that program evaluations, when combined with efforts to collect information, can be a positive step toward greater understanding of programs' effectiveness.

HUD's Assistant Secretary for Public and Indian Housing expressed concern regarding our reference on the highlights page of the report to the Indian CDBG program as one of 19 economic development programs that failed to meet their entrepreneurial performance goals. She stated that the entire program may be unfairly perceived as ineffective as a result of this statement. Our report states that 33 of 52 programs we examined set goals related to entrepreneurial assistance and that 19 of these 33 programs did not meet any of their goals or only met some of their goals. Our report does not state that these 19 programs were ineffective. We added language on the highlights page of the report to clarify that our findings were only based on each program's goals related to entrepreneurial assistance.

The Assistant Secretary also stated that our report misrepresents the Indian CDBG program as an economic development program. She noted that while economic development is an eligible program activity, only 3 percent of the dollars awarded under the program since 2005 funded economic development activities. She further noted that most of the program's grants were used for community development activities, such as building community buildings, developing infrastructure of various types, and rehabilitating housing units on Indian lands. As noted in our report, the 52 programs we examined for this report typically fund a variety of activities in addition to supporting entrepreneurs. In addition, the report notes that most of these programs either target or exclusively serve particular types of businesses.

The Assistant Secretary noted that an independent evaluation of the Indian CDBG program was conducted in 2006. HUD had not previously provided us with this evaluation. We revised our report to state that the Indian CDBG program had been evaluated within the past 12 years. Finally, the Assistant Secretary stated that HUD supports efforts to accurately measure the performance of its programs. She noted that HUD's Office of Native American Programs had recognized limitations in its method of projecting and measuring performance in the Indian CDBG program. She also stated that the office had begun drafting a revised form to be used at grant application and grant closeout to better collect performance measurement data, and that the office was examining its data collection procedures as well as the methodology used to establish program targets. These actions are consistent with our recommendation that the agencies collect program information and use it to help administer their programs.

USDA's Under Secretary for Rural Development stated that he agreed with our report's statements that entrepreneurs play a vital role in the U.S. economy and that no duplication exists among federal programs that assist entrepreneurs. However, he disagreed with some of the other observations in our report. First, he stated that our report broadly portrays federal programs that assist entrepreneurs and does not highlight the unique characteristics of each agency, such as USDA's Rural Development's specialization in rural economic development and its network of state and local area offices. Our report notes that most of USDA's 13 programs that can support entrepreneurs are limited to areas with a rural statutory definition. We also include discussion based on our outreach to participants in rural economic development, including regional commissions and authorities, on their experiences with the four federal agencies in rural economic development efforts. More importantly, however, when considering the unique characteristics of the various programs, we emphasize the need for agencies to conduct program evaluations to assess effectiveness. While the Under Secretary suggests that the rural focus and the network of state and local area offices enhance program effectiveness, USDA has not conducted evaluations to support this conclusion.

Second, USDA's Under Secretary stated that our report highlights examples where entrepreneurs may be eligible for multiple federal programs based on an entrepreneur's specific characteristics, but that the report does not mention whether this was a pervasive or problematic issue. He stated that rural entrepreneurs may be eligible for multiple programs, and that a business's unique situation dictates which programs best meets its needs. Again, our report emphasizes the need for evaluations to determine the relative effectiveness of different programs serving similar purposes. Third, regarding our findings related to the information agencies collect on program activities, the Under Secretary cited a number of tools that the Rural Business-Cooperative Service (RBS) uses to identify and improve the effectiveness of its programs. As noted in this report, we determined that USDA collected detailed information on the industry of each of the entrepreneurs it supports for all of its programs. In addition, we determined that USDA collected detailed information (19 categories) on how entrepreneurs use proceeds provided through 5 of its financial programs. However, we found that over the past 12 years USDA had conducted a program evaluation for only 1 of its 13 programs that can support entrepreneurs, including USDA programs that RBS does not administer.

Finally, the Under Secretary stated that the recommendations in our report are not explicit, which makes it unclear how RBS would effectively address them. Our report does provide information on how agencies could address our recommendations. First, we recommended that OMB, Commerce, HUD, SBA, and USDA work together to identify opportunities to enhance collaboration among programs, both within and across agencies. Our report identifies several practices that can help agencies and their offices enhance and sustain collaboration, which include indentifying common outcomes, establishing joint strategies, leveraging resources, determining roles and responsibilities, and developing compatible policies and procedures, among others. Second, we recommended that Commerce, HUD, USDA and SBA consistently collect information that would enable them to track the specific type of assistance provided and the entrepreneurs they serve and use this information to help administer their programs. Our report identifies programs that Commerce, HUD, SBA, and USDA administer for which the agencies did and did not maintain information in a readily available format that could be tracked to help administer the programs. Finally, we recommended that Commerce, HUD, SBA, and USDA conduct more evaluations to better understand why programs have not met performance goals and their overall effectiveness. Our report acknowledges that program evaluations can be costly; however, the report also notes that there are various methods agencies can employ to make the evaluations more cost-effective, such as relying on their own data instead of purchasing data from a vendor.

We are sending copies of this report to the appropriate congressional committees and other interested parties. In addition, this report will be available at no charge on the GAO website at http://www.gao.gov. Should you or your staff have any questions concerning this report, please contact William B. Shear, at (202) 512-8678, or shearw@gao.gov. Contact points for our Offices of Congressional Relations and Public Affairs may be found on the last page of this report. Key contributors to this report are listed in appendix IX.

William B. Shear
Director
Financial Markets
   and Community Investments

List of Congressional Committees

The Honorable Debbie Stabenow
Chair
The Honorable Pat Roberts
Ranking Member
Committee on Agriculture, Nutrition, and Forestry
United States Senate

The Honorable Kent Conrad
Chairman
The Honorable Jeff Sessions
Ranking Member
Committee on the Budget
United States Senate

The Honorable Barbara Boxer
Chair
The Honorable James M. Inhofe
Ranking Member
Committee on Environment and Public Works
United States Senate

The Honorable Mary Landrieu
Chair
The Honorable Olympia J. Snowe
Ranking Member
Committee on Small Business and Entrepreneurship
United States Senate

The Honorable Mark Warner
Chairman
Task Force on Government Performance
Committee on the Budget
United States Senate

The Honorable Paul Ryan
Chairman
The Honorable Chris Van Hollen
Ranking Member
Committee on the Budget
House of Representatives

The Honorable Spencer Bachus
Chair
The Honorable Barney Frank
Ranking Member
Committee on Financial Services
House of Representatives

The Honorable Darrell E. Issa
Chair
The Honorable Elijah Cummings
Ranking Member
Committee on Oversight and Government Reform
House of Representatives

The Honorable Sam Graves
Chair
The Honorable Nydia Velazquez
Ranking Member
Committee on Small Business
House of Representatives

The Honorable Timothy V. Johnson
Chairman
Subcommittee on Rural Development, Research,
  Biotechnology, and Foreign Agriculture
Committee on Agriculture
House of Representatives

Appendix I: Objectives, Scope and Methodology

This report discusses (1) the extent of overlap, fragmentation, and duplication and their effects on entrepreneurs, and agencies' actions to address them; and (2) the extent to which agencies collect information necessary to track program activities and whether these programs have met their performance goals and been evaluated.

To determine the extent of overlap and fragmentation among federal programs that fund economic development activities, we focused our analyses on 52 programs administered by the Departments of Agriculture (USDA), Commerce, and Housing and Urban Development (HUD) and the Small Business Administration (SBA) that are authorized to support entrepreneurs. Based on past work, these programs appeared to overlap the most within the four agencies with missions focused on economic development. We reviewed the statutes and regulations that authorize the activities that can be conducted under each program. We categorized the types of activities into three categories: (1) technical assistance, (2) financial assistance, and (3) government contracting assistance. Many of the programs can provide more than one type of assistance, and most focus on technical assistance, financial assistance, or both. To identify the effects of overlap and fragmentation on entrepreneurs and agencies' actions to address them, we focused on 35 of the 52 programs that provide technical assistance because there was significant overlap and fragmentation among these programs. We reviewed agency documents, such as inter-agency agreements, and conducted interviews to determine how technical assistance is provided to entrepreneurs, including the extent of agency collaboration at the local level. More specifically, we interviewed technical assistance providers, including 14 federal agency officials from four federal agencies located in the field, nine officials from two regional commissions, and 14 representatives of intermediaries (that is, third-party technical assistance providers); four entrepreneurs who have received assistance federal support; and five state and local partners in three geographic areas. These geographic areas included both urban and rural areas. We selected geographic areas based on, the presence of an active regional commission and evidence of collaboration among at least two of the four federal agencies being located within the same region. We assessed this technical assistance information against promising collaborative practices that we have previously identified.[1]

---

[1]GAO, *Results-Oriented Government: Practices That Can Help Enhance and Sustain Collaboration among Federal Agencies*, GAO-06-15 (Washington, D.C.: Oct. 21, 2005).

To determine the extent to which agencies collect information necessary
to track program activities, we reviewed agency manuals and data
collection forms that describe information collected on program activities
and methods for analyzing and using the information. Specifically, we
assessed each agency's capacity to track specific types of
entrepreneurial assistance they provided to specific types of beneficiaries,
as well as their ability to report this information in a readily available
format at the program level. We compared these processes against
standards for internal controls we have previously identified to determine
how well agencies track the support they provide to entrepreneurs.[2] To
determine the extent to which these 52 economic development programs
have met their performance goals, we reviewed agency documents on
their fiscal year 2011 program goals and accomplishments. We also
interviewed agency officials to determine reasons why goals were not met
(see app. III).

To describe results from program evaluations related to the effectiveness
of the 52 economic development programs that we reviewed, we
requested all studies that have been conducted on these programs from
the four agencies that administer the programs. Our document request
resulted in 19 studies. We refined the list of 19 studies by choosing to
focus on studies that were published in or after 2000. The resulting list of
program evaluations totaled 16. Because some evaluations studied more
than one program, these 16 evaluations covered 20 of the 52 programs in
our review. We reviewed the methodologies of these studies to ensure
that they were sound and determined that they were sufficiently reliable
for our purpose, which was to report high-level findings related to the
program's overall effectiveness (see app. V). Other evaluations of these
programs may exist.

To provide illustrative examples of each of the nine economic activities
related to economic development that we previously identified (see app. II),
we conducted a review of the literature that has been published in the past

---

[2]GAO, *Standards for Internal Control in the Federal Government*, GAO/AIMD-00-21.3.1
(Washington, D.C.: Nov. 1999).

5 years.[3] This review included publications from a variety of sources, including academic journals and trade publications. These sources contained examples of how these economic activities were being conducted at the national, state, and local levels in the United States. The list of examples we developed is not meant to be comprehensive but is intended to provide a range of economic activities that could be funded by federal programs.

We also used these nine economic activities to identify additional federal programs that may be able to fund at least one of the activities (these programs are listed in app. IV). During previous reviews, we focused on federal programs at Commerce, HUD, SBA, and USDA because these agencies have missions focused on economic development. For this report, we identified additional federal programs that could fund the nine economic activities. While many of the agencies that administer these additional programs do not have missions that focus on economic development, their programs may be able to fund at least one of the nine economic activities. We reviewed information on all programs contained in the 2011 Catalog of Federal Domestic Assistance (CFDA) and provided the list of programs to all of the administering agencies.[4] This list of additional federal programs may not be comprehensive because not all agencies provide data to CFDA (see app. IV).

---

[3]The nine economic activities are supporting entrepreneurial efforts, supporting business incubators and accelerators, constructing and renovating commercial buildings, constructing and renovating industrial parks and buildings, strategic planning and research, marketing and access to new markets for products and industries, supporting telecommunications and broadband infrastructure, supporting physical infrastructure, and supporting tourism.

[4]We have previously identified incomplete or inaccurate data in the CFDA, but we chose to rely on it for our purposes in this report because it is the only source that contains information on programs from many different federal agencies. We did not assess the data reliability of the CFDA. OMB has compiled initial lists of agencies and programs that contribute to crosscutting goals, as required by GPRAMA, on performance.gov, including those related to the entrepreneurship and small business goal. However, OMB noted that this was not meant to be comprehensive of all programs with any contribution to the crosscutting goals, and that they are continuing to update these lists.

We conducted this performance audit from June 2011 to July 2012 in accordance with generally accepted government auditing standards. Those standards require that we plan and perform the audit to obtain sufficient, appropriate evidence to provide a reasonable basis for our findings and conclusions based on our audit objectives. We believe that the evidence obtained provides a reasonable basis for our findings and conclusions based on our audit objectives.

Appendix II: Illustrative Examples of Economic Activities

In September 2000, we reported that there is no commonly accepted definition for economic development.[1] Absent a common definition for economic development, we subsequently developed a list of nine activities most often associated with economic development.[2] In general, we focused on economic activities that directly affected the overall development of an area, such as job creation and economic growth, rather than on activities that improved individuals' quality of life, such as housing and education. We previously relied on these economic activities to identify 80 economic development programs administered by the U.S. Departments of Agriculture (USDA), Commerce, and Housing and Urban Development (HUD) and the Small Business Administration (SBA) because these agencies have missions that focus on economic development.[3] In this report, we identified illustrative examples of each of the nine economic activities.

Illustrative Examples of Economic Activities

The following examples, which resulted from a review we conducted of academic journals and trade publications, illustrate a range of activities that could be supported by programs that can fund at least one of the economic activities. Examples include projects that are both publicly and privately funded, with many receiving funding from multiple sources in both sectors. They also had an explicit or implicit economic development goal, such as job creation or economic growth.

1. *Supporting entrepreneurial efforts.* This activity is the focus of this report, with programs grouped according to at least one of three types of assistance that address different entrepreneurial needs: help obtaining (1) technical assistance, which includes business training and counseling and research and development support; (2) financial assistance, which includes grants, loans, and venture capital; and (3) government contracts, which involves helping entrepreneurs qualify for federal procurement opportunities. Illustrative examples of this activity include the following initiatives:

---

[1]GAO, *Economic Development: Multiple Federal Programs Fund Similar Economic Development Activities*, GAO/RCED/GGD-00-220 (Washington, D.C.: Sept. 29, 2000).

[2]GAO, *Rural Economic Development: More Assurance Is Needed That Grant Funding Information Is Accurately Reported*, GAO-06-294 (Washington, D.C.: Feb. 24, 2006).

[3]GAO-11-318SP, GAO-11-477R and GAO-12-342SP.

- Individuals in an Iowa community formed an association of entrepreneurs to provide a broad range of services to entrepreneurs, including technical assistance in the form of mentor counseling, training sessions on various topics, and hosting conferences.

- A California community provided both financial and technical support to local small businesses in order to redevelop a business district. Businesses received micro-grants—small grants of $5,000 each—and were also required to participate in free workshops designed to give them additional tools and resources to succeed in a challenging marketplace. These workshops were produced by an SBA-funded Small Business Development Center.

- Iowa provided financial assistance to entrepreneurs through loan guarantees and a publicly funded limited liability corporation that could coordinate venture capital investments. The initiative was designed to increase capital levels and stimulate the creation of more local seed funds.

2. *Supporting business incubators and accelerators.* This activity can include all of the elements of entrepreneurial efforts, but combines these types of assistance with a facility that supports multiple businesses and may provide shared access to office space, technology, and other support services. Illustrative examples of this activity include the following initiatives:

- A technology business incubator was established at a Florida university so its faculty and service partners can provide business opportunities to client companies. The facility has grown to support a number of services to assist start-up businesses, including office and laboratory space, educational programs, and networking and mentoring opportunities with other experienced entrepreneurs.

- An Ohio community created a business accelerator that is designed to assist small, established companies, rather than businesses in their infancy, in becoming financially viable and creating jobs in the region. This facility includes office space, access to technology, and a variety of support services. The accelerator also collaborates with a center funded by SBA's Small Business Development Centers program and a local community college, which provide coaching and mentoring sessions, business plan reviews, workshops, training, referrals, and assistance in obtaining capital.

- An economic development organization in Pennsylvania created a network of business incubators and accelerators focused on developing and commercializing technology to create high-paying, sustainable jobs. The initiative supports early-stage and established companies with funding, support services, and a network of experts in related industries and academia.

3. *Constructing and renovating commercial buildings.* This activity can include support for the construction and renovation of buildings established for commercial purposes, such as for retail and office space. Illustrative examples of this activity include the following initiatives:

- A community in Iowa renovated a historic building that used to be a store to attract a large technology firm's service center. The renovations were designed to meet the firm's sustainability vision and were financed by public and private sources.

- A community in Arizona renovated a high school to create a new research laboratory. Further buildings were constructed in the area around this project to create a biomedical campus for both commercial and academic purposes.

- A community in Iowa renovated buildings in a historic millwork district to create urban mixed-use developments, which are designed to attract both commercial and residential activity.

4. *Constructing and renovating industrial parks and buildings.* This activity can include support for the construction and renovation of buildings and campuses established for industrial purposes, such as for manufacturing. Illustrative examples of this activity include the following initiatives:

- A public-private partnership in Nevada constructed an industrial park with new access to a freeway and energy infrastructure. The facility was zoned for heavy industry and designed to be away from population centers.

- A community in Massachusetts administered the transition of a former military base into a light industrial area focused on

sustainable development and attracted both small and large firms
to the redeveloped area.

- A public-private partnership in a North Carolina created several
  multi-jurisdictional business parks intended to improve local
  economies. These parks serve a number of industrial purposes,
  including technology, manufacturing, distribution, and logistics.
  Local governments obtained funding to conduct site evaluations
  and certification through Commerce's Economic Development
  Administration and HUD's Community Development Block Grant
  program.

5. *Strategic planning and research*. This activity includes plans for
   recruiting new businesses or industry clusters, economic research
   and analyses, and regional coordination and planning across
   jurisdictions and sectors. Illustrative examples of this activity include
   the following initiatives:

   - Local officials in a southeastern state formed a regional economic
     development organization to better coordinate economic and
     workforce development. The organization engages in marketing
     and recruitment of businesses and fosters partnerships between
     various public- and private-sector entities in the region.

   - A California community developed a plan for a business district to
     create jobs and produce savings for businesses. The plan defined
     resources, timeframes, and types of assistance needed to execute
     this strategy.

   - A regional consortium operating in areas of two southern states
     conducted research on their area's economic strengths and
     developed an action plan to leverage these strengths. Research
     included the identification of industry clusters that could be well
     suited to the area.

6. *Marketing and access to new markets for products and industries*.
   This activity may include marketing of both new and existing products
   and industries, facilitating access to new markets, and supporting new
   uses for existing products. Illustrative examples of this activity include
   the following initiatives:

   - A publicly funded regional technology center in New York provides
     a range of resources for local manufacturing and technology

companies, including assistance with developing sales and growth
strategies, conducting marketing activities for increased market
share and revenue in existing or new markets, and identifying new
customers and market niches.

- A regional economic development organization in North Carolina
formed an energy industry cluster that included a bio-energy
facility where businesses are colocated with a landfill. These
businesses are able to sell what were formerly waste products in
new markets, such as alternative fuels and wood pallets.

- Several southern and Midwestern states have leveraged federal
and state funds to assist rural businesses with e-commerce
strategies, including assistance reaching global markets and
strengthening competitive market advantages. Both USDA and
Commerce provided some funding for this initiative.

7. *Supporting telecommunications and broadband infrastructure.* This
activity may include building, refurbishing, and enhancing
infrastructure used to expand access and improve the speed and
reliability of Internet access, wireless phone services, and other
electronic communication methods. Illustrative examples of this
activity include the following initiatives:

- A public-private partnership in a city in Ohio provides businesses
and residents with an underground conduit network that supports
multiple fiber-based systems for voice, data, and video
communications, intended to provide high-speed access to the
global marketplace.

- A multi-state rural regional development organization in the
southwestern United States coordinated the construction of a
broadband Internet network that was intended to generate new
opportunities for economic development. The initiative was funded
by both private and public investments and covered a large
geographic area.

- Regional leaders collaborated with a state commission to expand
broadband infrastructure to businesses, schools, and industrial
parks in a Virginia city. The high-speed network is noted to be
comparable to or faster than that of any other metropolitan area of
the country, is available at a relatively low cost, and is intended to
attract businesses to the area.

8. *Supporting physical infrastructure*. This activity includes constructing and repairing infrastructure related to (1) transportation, such as roads, airports and rail; (2) water and sewer; (3) energy; and (4) other amenities, such as pedestrian areas, parking, and beautification projects. Illustrative examples of this activity include the following initiatives:

- A community in New York is planning to renovate a business district by creating new rail service, a pedestrian mall, and green space.

- A community in Ohio renovated their underdeveloped downtown area by constructing better roads and pedestrian space, improving green space, and moving power lines underground. The project was part of a plan to reduce blight and make the area more accessible for visitors.

- A community in North Carolina renovated a vacant textile manufacturing space and downtown area to create a scientific research campus, facilitating this work through water line replacements, the addition of a pedestrian tunnel, and road improvements.

9. *Supporting tourism*. This activity includes marketing, infrastructure improvement, planning, and research specifically related to developing and improving tourism, as well as supporting special events and festivals to attract visitors. Illustrative examples of this activity include the following initiatives:

- A community in Kentucky improved trails in natural areas to attract tourists for horseback riding and other recreational uses. In addition to trail improvements, the community utilized survey research, marketing, and special events to draw visitors to the area.

- A community in North Carolina entered into public-private partnerships to construct a cluster of tourist venues that included sports and arts museums, an arena, convention center, and performing arts venues. The community utilized a strategic plan for development and a branded name to market the area.

- A county in Mississippi partnered with other regional entities to market their gaming industry and other amenities as part of a broader regional campaign. This new partnership promoted region-wide tourism and focused on key markets that the area may draw visitors from.

Appendix III: Performance Goals and Accomplishments for 52 Programs that Can Support Entrepreneurs, Fiscal Year 2011

Agency	Program Name and Mission	Fiscal year 2011 Obligations[a]	Performance Measures	Fiscal year 2011 Performance Goal	Fiscal year 2011 Actual Performance[b]	Met Individual Goals	Met All Goals
Department of Commerce (Commerce) – Economic Development Administration (EDA)[c]	Grants for Public Works and Economic Development Facilities Supports the construction or rehabilitation of essential public infrastructure and facilities necessary to support job creation, attract private-sector capital, and promote regional competitiveness, innovation, and entrepreneurship, including investments that expand and upgrade infrastructure to attract new industry, support technology-led development, accelerate new business development, and enhance the ability of regions to capitalize on opportunities presented by free trade.	$114,529,000	Private investment leveraged (3, 6, and 9 years after award)	Private investment leveraged–9 year totals (in millions): $1,940 Private investment leveraged–6 year totals (in millions): $674 Private investment leveraged–3 year totals (in millions): $244.6	Private investment leveraged–9 year totals (in millions): $3,960 Private investment leveraged–6 year totals (in millions): $1,617 Private investment leveraged–3 year totals (in millions): $1,475	Yes	Partial
Commerce EDA	Grants for Public Works and Economic Development Facilities		Total jobs created/retained (3, 6, and 9 years after award)	Jobs created/retained –9 year totals: 57,800 Jobs created/retained –6 year totals: 18,193 Jobs created/retained –3 year totals: 6,256	Jobs created/retained–9 year totals: 56,058 Jobs created/retained–6 year totals: 26,416 Jobs created/retained–3 year totals: 14,842	Partial	

Appendix III: Performance Goals and Accomplishments for 52 Programs that Can Support Entrepreneurs, Fiscal Year 2011

Agency	Program Name and Mission	Fiscal year 2011 Obligations[a]	Performance Measures	Fiscal year 2011 Performance Goal	Fiscal year 2011 Actual Performance[b]	Met Individual Goals	Met All Goals
Commerce EDA	Economic Adjustment Assistance Supports economically distressed communities in their ability to compete economically by stimulating private investment and promoting job creation in targeted areas. Current investment priorities include proposals that foster innovation and enhance regions' global economic competitiveness by supporting existing industry clusters, developing emerging new clusters, or attracting new regional economic drivers.	$78,720,000	Private investment leveraged (3, 6, and 9 years after award)	Private investment leveraged–9 year totals (in millions): $1,940 Private investment leveraged–6 year totals (in millions): $674 Private investment leveraged–3 year totals (in millions): $244.6	Private investment leveraged–9 year totals (in millions): $3,960 Private investment leveraged–6 year totals (in millions): $1,617 Private investment leveraged–3 year totals (in millions): $1,475	Yes	Partial
Commerce EDA	Economic Adjustment Assistance		Total jobs created/retained (3, 6, and 9 years after award)	Jobs created/retained– 9 year totals: 57,800 Jobs created/retained– 6 year totals: 18,193 Jobs created/retained– 3 year totals: 6,256	Jobs created/retained– 9 year totals: 56,058 Jobs created/retained– 6 year totals: 26,416 Jobs created/retained– 3 year totals: 14,842	Partial	
Commerce EDA	Global Climate Change Mitigation Incentive Fund Supports economic development projects that create jobs through, and increase private capital investment in, efforts to limit the nation's dependence on fossil fuels, enhance energy efficiency, curb greenhouse gas emissions, and protect natural systems. The program helps to cultivate innovations that can fuel "green growth" in communities suffering from economic distress.	$17,466,000	Private investment leveraged (3, 6, and 9 years after award)	Private investment leveraged–9 year totals (in millions): $1,940 Private investment leveraged–6 year totals (in millions): $674 Private investment leveraged–3 year totals (in millions): $244.6	Private investment leveraged–9 year totals (in millions): $3,960 Private investment leveraged–6 year totals (in millions): $1,617 Private investment leveraged–3 year totals (in millions): $1,475	Yes	Partial
Commerce EDA	Global Climate Change Mitigation Incentive Fund		Total jobs created/retained (3, 6, and 9 years after award)	Jobs created/retained– 9 year totals: 57,800 Jobs created/retained– 6 year totals: 18,193 Jobs created/retained– 3 year totals: 6,256	Jobs created/ retained– 9 year totals: 56,058 Jobs created/ retained– 6 year totals: 26,416 Jobs created/ retained– 3 year totals: 14,842	Partial	

GAO-12-819 Entrepreneurial Assistance

Appendix III: Performance Goals and Accomplishments for 52 Programs that Can Support Entrepreneurs, Fiscal Year 2011

Agency	Program Name and Mission	Fiscal year 2011 Obligations[a]	Performance Measures	Fiscal year 2011 Performance Goal	Fiscal year 2011 Actual Performance[b]	Met Individual Goals	Met All Goals
Commerce EDA	Economic Development/Technical Assistance Provides focused assistance to public and nonprofit leaders to help in economic development decision making (e.g., project planning, impact analyses, feasibility studies). The program also supports the University Center Economic Development Program, which makes the resources of universities available to the economic development community.	$13,373,000	Percentage of University Center clients taking action as a result of the assistance facilitated	75%	68%	No	Partial
Commerce EDA	Economic Development/Technical Assistance		Percentage of those actions taken by University Center clients that achieved expected results	80%	83%	Yes	
Commerce EDA	Economic Development/Support for Planning Organizations Provides planning assistance to provide support to Planning Organizations (as defined in 13 CFR 303.2) for the development, implementation, revision, or replacement of a Comprehensive Economic Development Strategy, short-term planning efforts, and state plans designed to create and retain higher-skill, higher-wage jobs, particularly for the unemployed and underemployed in the nation's most economically distressed regions.	$31,352,000	Percentage of economic development districts and Indian tribes implementing economic development projects from the comprehensive economic development strategy that lead to private investment and jobs	95%	86%	No	No
Commerce EDA	Economic Development/Support for Planning Organizations		Percentage of substate jurisdiction members actively participating in the economic development district program	89%	85%	No	
Commerce EDA	Trade Adjustment Assistance (TAA) for Firms The program helps economically distressed U.S. businesses in building competitiveness strategies to increase	$15,418,000	Percentage of TAA Center clients taking action as a result of the assistance facilitated	90%	73%	No	Partial

Agency	Program Name and Mission	Fiscal year 2011 Obligations[a]	Performance Measures	Fiscal year 2011 Performance Goal	Fiscal year 2011 Actual Performance[b]	Met Individual Goals	Met All Goals
	exports and thereby create jobs. The program provides technical assistance to U.S. businesses that have lost sales and employment due to increased imports of similar or competitive goods and services. Technical assistance is provided through a nationwide network of eleven Economic Development Administration-funded Trade Adjustment Assistance Centers.						
Commerce EDA	Trade Adjustment Assistance for Firms		Percentage of actions taken by TAA Center clients that achieved expected results	95%	100%	Yes	
Commerce – Minority Business Development Agency (MDBA)	Native American Business Enterprise Centers (NABEC)[d] The program promotes the growth and competitiveness of businesses owned by Native Americans and eligible minorities. NABEC operators leverage project staff and professional consultants to provide a wide range of direct business assistance services to Native American tribal entities and eligible minority-owned firms. NABEC services include, but are not limited to, initial consultations and assessments, business technical assistance, and access to federal and nonfederal procurement and financing opportunities.	$0	Dollar value of contract awards obtained	$1.1 billion	$2.1 billion	Yes	Yes
Commerce MBDA	Native American Business Enterprise Centers		Dollar value of financial awards obtained	$0.9 billion	$1.8 billion	Yes	
Commerce MBDA	Native American Business Enterprise Centers		Number of jobs created	5,000	5,787	Yes	
Commerce MBDA	Minority Business Center (MBC) The program promotes the growth and competitiveness of eligible minority-owned businesses. MBC operators leverage project staff and professional	$17,948,122	Dollar value of contract awards obtained	$1.1 billion	$2.1 billion	Yes	Yes

Agency	Program Name and Mission	Fiscal year 2011 Obligations[a]	Performance Measures	Fiscal year 2011 Performance Goal	Fiscal year 2011 Actual Performance[b]	Met Individual Goals	Met All Goals
	consultants to provide a wide range of direct business assistance services to eligible minority-owned firms. Services include initial consultations and assessments, business technical assistance, and access to federal and nonfederal procurement and financing opportunities. MBDA currently funds a network of 30 MBC projects located throughout the United States.						
Commerce MBDA	Minority Business Center		Dollar value of financial awards obtained	$0.9 billion	$1.8 billion	Yes	
Commerce MBDA	Minority Business Center		Number of jobs created	5,000	5,787	Yes	
Department of Housing and Urban Development (HUD)	Community Development Block Grant (CDBG)/Insular Areas HUD annually allocates $7 million of CDBG funds to the Insular Areas program in proportion to the populations of the eligible territories. The program is administered by HUD's field offices in Puerto Rico and Hawaii. The CDBG programs allocate annual grants to develop viable communities by providing decent housing, a suitable living environment, and opportunities to expand economic opportunities, principally for low- and moderate-income persons.	$ 214,396[e]	Jobs created and retained	None	15,549	N/A	N/A
HUD	CDBG/Insular Areas		Businesses assisted	None	24,331	N/A	N/A
HUD	CDBG/Entitlement Grants The CDBG program works to ensure decent affordable housing, to provide services to the most vulnerable in our communities, and to create jobs through the expansion and retention of businesses. The CDBG entitlement program allocates annual grants to larger cities and urban counties to	$325,549,306[f]	Jobs created and retained	None	15,549	N/A	N/A

Agency	Program Name and Mission	Fiscal year 2011 Obligations[a]	Performance Measures	Fiscal year 2011 Performance Goal	Fiscal year 2011 Actual Performance[b]	Met Individual Goals	Met All Goals
	develop viable communities by providing decent housing, a suitable living environment, and opportunities to expand economic opportunities, principally for low- and moderate-income persons.						
HUD	CDBG/Entitlement Grants		Businesses assisted	None	24,331	N/A	
HUD	CDBG/States	$559,961,961[g]	Jobs created and retained	None	15,549	N/A	N/A
	The primary statutory objective of the CDBG States program is to develop viable communities by providing decent housing, a suitable living environment, and opportunities to expand economic opportunities, principally for low- and moderate-income persons. The state must ensure that at least 70 percent of its CDBG grant funds are used for activities that benefit low- and moderate-income persons over a 1-, 2-, or 3-year time period selected by the state.						
HUD	CDBG/States		Businesses assisted	None	24,331	N/A	
HUD	CDBG/Non-entitlement CDBG Grants in Hawaii	$338,257[h]	Jobs created and retained	None	15,549	N/A	N/A
	HUD continues to administer the program for the non-entitlement counties in the state of Hawaii because the state has permanently elected not to participate in the State CDBG program. The CDBG programs allocate annual grants to develop viable communities by providing decent housing, a suitable living environment, and opportunities to expand economic opportunities, principally for low- and moderate-income persons.						
HUD	CDBG/Non-entitlement CDBG Grants in Hawaii		Businesses assisted	None	24,331	N/A	

Agency	Program Name and Mission	Fiscal year 2011 Obligations[a]	Performance Measures	Fiscal year 2011 Performance Goal	Fiscal year 2011 Actual Performance[b]	Met Individual Goals	Met All Goals
HUD	CDBG/Section 108 Loan Guarantees Section 108 is the loan guarantee provision of the CDBG program. Section 108 provides communities with a source of financing for economic development, housing rehabilitation, public facilities, and large-scale physical development projects. It allows them to transform a small portion of their CDBG funds into federally guaranteed loans large enough to pursue physical and economic revitalization projects that can renew entire neighborhoods.	$6,000,000	Jobs proposed to be created or retained	None	7,306	N/A	N/A
HUD	CDBG/Brownfields Economic Development Initiative (BEDI) The purpose of the BEDI program is to spur the return of brownfields to productive economic use through financial assistance to public entities in the redevelopment of brownfields and enhance the security or improve the viability of a project financed with Section 108-guaranteed loan authority.	$0	Jobs proposed to be created or retained	3,157	2,409	No	No
HUD	CDBG Disaster Recovery Grants[l] Grantees may use CDBG Disaster Recovery funds for recovery efforts involving housing, economic development, infrastructure, and prevention of further damage to affected areas, if such use does not duplicate funding available from the Federal Emergency Management Agency, the Small Business Administration, and the U.S. Army Corps of Engineers. The mission and goals of the CDBG Disaster Recovery Grants program may be expanded or limited per the individual appropriation that it receives each year.	$0	Businesses assisted	None	N/A	N/A	N/A

Page 53

GAO-12-819 Entrepreneurial Assistance

Agency	Program Name and Mission	Fiscal year 2011 Obligations[a]	Performance Measures	Fiscal year 2011 Performance Goal	Fiscal year 2011 Actual Performance[b]	Met Individual Goals	Met All Goals
HUD	CDBG Disaster Recovery Grants		Permanent jobs created (tracked by low income, moderate income and total)	None	N/A	N/A	
HUD	CDBG Disaster Recovery Grants		Permanent jobs retained (tracked by low income, moderate income and total)	None	N/A	N/A	
HUD	CDBG Disaster Recovery Grants		Number of buildings (nonresidential) assisted	None	N/A	N/A	
HUD	Section 4 Capacity Building for Affordable Housing and Community Development Through funding of national intermediaries, the Section 4 Capacity Building program enhances the capacity and ability of community development corporations and community housing development organizations to carry out community development and affordable housing activities and to attract private investment for housing, economic development, and other community revitalization activities that benefit low-income families.	$50,000,000	Number of trainings created and provided to Community Development Corporations (CDC)	794	Not reported	Unknown	Unknown
HUD	Section 4 Capacity Building for Affordable Housing and Community Development		Development cost estimates of community development projects funded by CDCs	$988 million	Not reported	Unknown	
HUD	Section 4 Capacity Building for Affordable Housing and Community Development		Number of homes renovated, preserved or newly constructed	6,060	Not reported	Unknown	
HUD	Section 4 Capacity Building for Affordable Housing and Community Development		Efficiency measure of per-unit cost of capacity building for housing units developed or renovated	None	N/A	N/A	
HUD	Rural Innovation Fund[j] The Rural Innovation Fund program was established to improve the quality of life for residents of distressed rural areas by supporting innovative and catalytic economic development and housing	$0[k]	Number of full-time and part-time jobs created	None	N/A	N/A	N/A

programs. The program is designed to support

(1) job creation through business development and expansion,

(2) investment in human capital through job training and education; and

(3) expanding the supply of affordable housing with access to job centers or transportation.

Rural Innovation Fund grantees are selected through a competitive process.

Agency	Program Name and Mission	Fiscal year 2011 Obligations[a]	Performance Measures	Fiscal year 2011 Performance Goal	Fiscal year 2011 Actual Performance[b]	Met Individual Goals	Met All Goals
HUD	Rural Innovation Fund		Number of persons receiving job training	None	N/A	N/A	
HUD	Rural Innovation Fund		Number of new businesses opened	None	N/A	N/A	
HUD	Rural Innovation Fund		Number of affordable housing units constructed	None	N/A	N/A	
HUD	Rural Innovation Fund		Number of residents receiving homeownership counseling	None	N/A	N/A	
HUD	Hispanic-Serving Institutions Assisting Communities

The Hispanic-Serving Institutions Assisting Communities program helps Hispanic-Serving Institutions expand their role and effectiveness in addressing community development needs in their localities, including revitalization, housing, and economic development, principally for persons of low and moderate income. Accredited Hispanic-Serving Institutions of higher education that provide 2- and 4-year degrees are eligible to participate in this program. For an institution to qualify as a Hispanic-Serving Institution, at least 25 percent of the undergraduate enrollment must be Hispanic students. | $0 | None | N/A | N/A | N/A | N/A |

Agency	Program Name and Mission	Fiscal year 2011 Obligations[a]	Performance Measures	Fiscal year 2011 Performance Goal	Fiscal year 2011 Actual Performance[b]	Met Individual Goals	Met All Goals
HUD	Alaska Native/Native Hawaiian Institutions Assisting Communities The Alaska Native/Native Hawaiian Institutions program helps these institutions expand their role and effectiveness in addressing community development needs in their localities, including revitalization, housing, and economic development, principally for persons of low and moderate income. The program encourages colleges and universities to integrate community engagement themes into their curriculum, academic studies, and student activities.	$0	None	N/A	N/A	N/A	N/A
HUD	Indian CDBG The purpose of the Indian CDBG program is the development of viable Indian and Alaska Native communities, including the creation of decent housing, suitable living environments, and economic opportunities primarily for persons with low and moderate incomes as defined in 24 CFR 1003.4. Funds may be used to improve housing stock, provide community facilities, improve infrastructure, and expand job opportunities by supporting the economic development of the communities in some instances.	$64,000,000	Jobs created	24	0	No	No
HUD	Indian CDBG		Rehabilitated housing units	701	409	No	
HUD	Indian CDBG		Constructed community buildings	49	30	No	
HUD	Indian CDBG		Average cost per community building	None	N/A	N/A	
HUD	Indian CDBG		Average amount of Indian CDBG dollars spent per housing unit rehabilitated	None	N/A	N/A	
Small	7(a) Loan Program	$88,000,000	Loan dollars approved	$12.8 billion	$19.7 billion	Yes	Yes

GAO-12-819 Entrepreneurial Assistance

Agency	Program Name and Mission	Fiscal year 2011 Obligations[a]	Performance Measures	Fiscal year 2011 Performance Goal	Fiscal year 2011 Actual Performance[b]	Met Individual Goals	Met All Goals
Business Administration (SBA)	The 7(a) Loan Program is SBA's primary program for helping start-up and existing small businesses, with financing guaranteed for a variety of general business purposes. 7(a) loans are the most basic and most commonly used type of loans. They are also the most flexible, since financing can be guaranteed for a variety of general business purposes, including working capital, machinery and equipment, furniture and fixtures, land and building (including purchase, renovation and new construction), leasehold improvements, and debt refinancing (under special conditions).						
SBA	7(a) Loan Program		Small businesses assisted	40,700	46,749	Yes	
SBA	7(a) Loan Program		Jobs supported	474,100	582,707	Yes	
SBA	7(a) Loan Program		Active lending partners	3,000	3,537	Yes	
SBA	7(a) Loan Program		Underserved markets– small businesses assisted	24,800	28,389	Yes	
SBA	7(a) Loan Program		Cost per small business assisted	None	$1,882	N/A	
SBA	504 Loan Program The 504 Loan Program provides growing businesses with long-term, fixed-rate financing for major fixed assets, such as land and buildings. A typical 504 project includes a loan secured from a private-sector lender with a senior lien covering up to 50 percent of the project cost, a loan secured from a Certified Development Company (backed by a 100 percent SBA-guaranteed debenture) with a junior lien covering up to 40 percent of the total cost, and a contribution from the borrower of at least 10 percent equity.	$38,888,000	Loan dollars approved	$4.8 billion	$4.8 billion	Yes	Partial
SBA	504 Loan Program		Small businesses assisted	8,100	7,752	No	

Appendix III: Performance Goals and Accomplishments for 52 Programs that Can Support Entrepreneurs, Fiscal Year 2011

Agency	Program Name and Mission	Fiscal year 2011 Obligations[a]	Performance Measures	Fiscal year 2011 Performance Goal	Fiscal year 2011 Actual Performance[b]	Met Individual Goals	Met All Goals
SBA	504 Loan Program		Jobs supported	88,800	87,337	No	
SBA	504 Loan Program		Underserved market – small businesses assisted	4,800	4,548	No	
SBA	504 Loan Program		Active lending partners	267	249	No	
SBA	504 Loan Program		Cost per small business assisted	None	$5,017	N/A	
SBA	Microloan Program	$38,729,000	Small businesses assisted	4,600	3,999	No	Partial
	SBA's Microloan Program provides small businesses with small, short-term loans for working capital or the purchase of inventory, supplies, furniture, fixtures, machinery or equipment. SBA makes funds available to specially designated intermediary lenders, which are nonprofit organizations with experience in lending and technical assistance. These intermediaries then make loans to eligible borrowers in amounts up to a maximum of $50,000.						
SBA	Microloan Program		Jobs supported	14,500	13,271	No	
SBA	Microloan Program		Loans approved by microlenders	$65 million	$47 million	No	
SBA	Microloan Program		Businesses Counseled	6,500	15,900	Yes	
SBA	Microloan Program		Underserved markets– small businesses assisted	4,600	3,999	No	
SBA	Microloan Program		Active lending partners	126	121	No	
SBA	Microloan Program		Cost per small business assisted	None	$9,685	N/A	
SBA	Surety Bond Guarantee Program	$4,865,000	Contract value of bid and final bonds	$3.3 billion	$3.7 billion	Yes	Yes
	SBA provides and manages surety bond guarantees for qualified small and emerging businesses through the Surety Bond Guarantee Program. Participating sureties receive guarantees that SBA will assume a predetermined percentage of loss in the event the contractor should breach the terms of the contract.						

GAO-12-819 Entrepreneurial Assistance

Agency	Program Name and Mission	Fiscal year 2011 Obligations[a]	Performance Measures	Fiscal year 2011 Performance Goal	Fiscal year 2011 Actual Performance[b]	Met Individual Goals	Met All Goals
SBA	Surety Bond Guarantee Program		Bid and final bonds guaranteed	7,600	8,638	Yes	
SBA	Surety Bond Guarantee Program		Jobs supported	6,400	17,421	Yes	
SBA	Surety Bond Guarantee Program		Cost per job supported	None	$279	N/A	
SBA	Program for Investment in Micro-Entrepreneurs (PRIME) PRIME provides assistance to various organizations. These organizations help low-income entrepreneurs who lack sufficient training and education to gain access to capital to establish and expand their small businesses.	$8,863,000	None	None	N/A	N/A	N/A
SBA	Small Business Development Centers (SBDC) SBDCs assist clients in gaining access to SBA loan programs and private capital to start up and expand their businesses. SBDC services are available to all small business populations. There are specialized programs for minorities, women, international trade, technology, energy efficiency, veterans, people with disabilities, and 8(a) firms in all stages, as well as individuals in low- and moderate-income urban and rural areas. The ultimate objective of the SBDC program is to support, strengthen, sustain, and grow local economies and business entities	$130,323,000	Long-term counseling clients	61,000	62, 117	Yes	Partial
SBA	Small Business Development Centers		Small businesses created	12,500	13,664	Yes	
SBA	Small Business Development Centers		Jobs supported	None	N/A	N/A	
SBA	Small Business Development Centers		Capital infusions	$3.7 billion	$3.6 billion	No	
SBA	Small Business Development Centers		Cost per job supported	None	N/A	N/A	
SBA	Small Business Development Centers		Cost per small business created	None	$9,538	N/A	

Agency	Program Name and Mission	Fiscal year 2011 Obligations[a]	Performance Measures	Fiscal year 2011 Performance Goal	Fiscal year 2011 Actual Performance[b]	Met Individual Goals	Met All Goals
SBA	Women's Business Centers (WBC) — WBCs provide long-term training as well as counseling and mentoring services. By statute, WBCs fill a gap by focusing on women who are socially and economically disadvantaged. WBCs offer classes during regular working hours as well as during the evenings and weekends to serve clients who work during the day. The WBCs often provide counseling in multiple languages.	$19,446,000	Small businesses assisted	135,000	138,923	Yes	Yes
SBA	Women's Business Centers		Small businesses created	618	701	Yes	
SBA	Women's Business Centers		Cost per small business assisted	None	$140	N/A	
SBA	SCORE — SCORE is a nonprofit association comprised of more than 13,000 volunteer business professionals in more than 350 chapters and on-line nationwide, dedicated to educating and assisting entrepreneurs and small business owners in the formation, growth, and expansion of their small businesses through mentoring, business advising and training.	$12,980,000	Small businesses assisted	349,867	356,837	Yes	Partial
SBA	SCORE		Small businesses created	1,082	816	No	
SBA	SCORE		Cost per small business assisted	None	$36.38	N/A	
SBA	Veterans Business Outreach Centers — The Veterans Business Outreach program is designed to provide entrepreneurial development services such as business training, counseling and mentoring, and referrals for eligible veterans owning or considering starting a small business.	$8,995,000	Veterans assisted	100,000	137,011	Yes	Yes
SBA	Veteran's Business Outreach Centers		Customer satisfaction	91%	91%	Yes	

Agency	Program Name and Mission	Fiscal year 2011 Obligations[a]	Performance Measures	Fiscal year 2011 Performance Goal	Fiscal year 2011 Actual Performance[b]	Met Individual Goals	Met All Goals
SBA	Veteran's Business Outreach Centers		Cost per veteran assisted	None	$65.65	N/A	
SBA	7(j) Technical Assistance The 7(j) program provides qualifying businesses with counseling and training in the areas of financing, business development, management, accounting, bookkeeping, marketing, and other small business operating concerns.	$6,502,000	Small businesses assisted	3,550	3,550	Yes	Yes
SBA	7(j) Technical Assistance		Cost per small business assisted	None	$1,832	N/A	
SBA	8(a) Business Development Program The 8(a) Business Development program provides various forms of assistance (management and technical assistance, government contracting assistance, and advocacy support) to foster the growth and development of businesses owned and controlled by socially and economically disadvantaged individuals. SBA assists these businesses, during their nine year tenure in the 8(a) Business Development program, in gaining equal access to the resources necessary to develop their businesses and improve their ability to compete.	$58,274,000	Small businesses assisted	9,457	7,814	No	No
SBA	8(a) Business Development Program		Cost per small business assisted	None	$7,458	N/A	
SBA	8(a) Business Development Program		Contracts to small disadvantaged businesses, which includes 8(a) program participants (%)	5%	Not reported	Unknown	
SBA	Historically Underutilized Business Zones (HUBZone) The HUBZone program helps small businesses located in both urban and rural communities gain preferential access to federal procurement opportunities. These preferences go to	$15,569,000	Small businesses assisted	4,000	5,801	Yes	Partial

GAO-12-819 Entrepreneurial Assistance

Agency	Program Name and Mission	Fiscal year 2011 Obligations[a]	Performance Measures	Fiscal year 2011 Performance Goal	Fiscal year 2011 Actual Performance[b]	Met Individual Goals	Met All Goals
	small businesses that obtain HUBZone certification in part by employing staff who live in a HUBZone. The company must also maintain a "principal office" in one of these specially designated areas.						
SBA	HUBZone		Annual value of federal contracts	$12 billion	$9.9 billion	No	
SBA	HUBZone		Cost per small businesses assisted	None	$2,684	N/A	
SBA	HUBZone		Cost per federal contract dollar	None	$.0015	N/A	
SBA	HUBZone		Contracts to HUBZone firms	3%	2.3%	No	
SBA	Procurement Assistance to Small Businesses The program assists small businesses in obtaining federal government contracts and subcontracts.	$21,171,000	Percent of federal prime and subcontracting dollars awarded to small businesses	For prime contracting, statutory goal is 23%; for subcontracting, there is no statutory goal, but SBA has set a goal of 35.9%.	21.65%	No	No
SBA	Small Business Innovation Research Program (SBIR) The SBIR program encourages small businesses to explore their technological potential and provides the incentive to profit from its commercialization. Each year, 11 federal departments and agencies are required by SBIR to reserve a portion of their research and development funds for awards to small businesses. SBA is the coordinating agency for the SBIR program. It directs the agencies' implementation of SBIR, reviews their progress, and reports annually to Congress on the program's operation.	$781,000	Commercialization / Innovation • Number of companies • Number of Phase II awards • Aggregate amount of SBIR award monies awarded to cohort • Aggregate sales/ revenue from cohort • Aggregate additional investment in cohort • Number of exits – Initial Public Offerings or Merger and Acquisition activity • Value of exits, in dollars	None	N/A	N/A	N/A

Agency	Program Name and Mission	Fiscal year 2011 Obligations[a]	Performance Measures	Fiscal year 2011 Performance Goal	Fiscal year 2011 Actual Performance[b]	Met Individual Goals	Met All Goals
			• Number of employees employed by awardees • Percent of awards that brought products to market (Note: Multiple awards may lead to only one product, but all awards should be given credit)				
SBA	SBIR		Women and Minorities • Percentage of awardees that are minority owned • Percentage of awardees that are women owned • Percentage of awardees that are HUBZone • Percentage of applicants that are minority owned that received an award • Percentage of applicants that are women owned that received an award	None	N/A	N/A	
SBA	SBIR		Efficiency and Effectiveness • Time between close of solicitation and selection • Time between selection and cash awarded • Total sum of time between close of solicitation and cash awarded	None	N/A	N/A	

Agency	Program Name and Mission	Fiscal year 2011 Obligations[a]	Performance Measures	Fiscal year 2011 Performance Goal	Fiscal year 2011 Actual Performance[b]	Met Individual Goals	Met All Goals
SBA	SBIR		Repeat-award winners <ul><li>Percentage of first-time Phase II awardees per year per agency</li><li>Percent age of first-time Phase I awardees per year per agency</li></ul>	None	N/A	N/A	N/A
SBA	Small Business Technology Transfer Program (STTR) The STTR program encourages small businesses to explore their technological potential and provides the incentive to profit from its commercialization. Each year, five federal agencies are required to reserve a portion of their research and development funds for awards to small businesses. SBA is the coordinating agency for the STTR program. It directs the agencies' implementation of STTR, reviews their progress, and reports annually to Congress on its operation. STTR requires cooperation with a university or approved research institution.	$352,000	Commercialization / Innovation <ul><li>Number of companies</li><li>Number of Phase II awards</li><li>Aggregate amount of SBIR award monies awarded to cohort</li><li>Aggregate sales/revenue from cohort</li><li>Aggregate additional investment in cohort</li><li>Number of exits – Initial Public Offerings or Merger and Acquisition activity</li><li>Value of exits, in dollars</li><li>Number of employees employed by awardees</li><li>Percent of awards that brought products to market (Note: Multiple awards may lead to only one product, but all awards should be given credit)</li></ul>	None	N/A	N/A	N/A

Agency	Program Name and Mission	Fiscal year 2011 Obligations[a]	Performance Measures	Fiscal year 2011 Performance Goal	Fiscal year 2011 Actual Performance[b]	Met Individual Goals	Met All Goals
SBA	STTR		Women and Minorities • Percentage of awardees that are minority owned • Percentage of awardees that are women owned • Percentage of awardees that are HUBZone • Percentage of applicants that are minority owned that received an award • Percentage of applicants that are women owned that received an award	None	N/A	N/A	
SBA	STTR		Efficiency and Effectiveness • Time between close of solicitation and selection • Time between selection and cash awarded • Total sum of time between close of solicitation and cash awarded	None	N/A	N/A	
SBA	STTR		Repeat-award winners • Percentage of first-time Phase II awardees per year per agency • Percentage of first-time Phase I awardees per year per agency	None	N/A	N/A	

Agency	Program Name and Mission	Fiscal year 2011 Obligations[a]	Performance Measures	Fiscal year 2011 Performance Goal	Fiscal year 2011 Actual Performance[b]	Met Individual Goals	Met All Goals
SBA	Small Business Investment Company (SBIC) Program The SBIC program aims to increase the availability of venture capital to small businesses. SBICs are privately owned and managed investment funds, licensed and regulated by SBA, that use their own capital plus funds borrowed with an SBA guarantee to make equity and debt investments in qualifying small businesses.	$26,305,000	Small business assisted	1,150	1,339	Yes	Yes
SBA	SBIC		Underserved markets— small businesses assisted	345	430	Yes	
SBA	SBIC		Amount of debenture leveraged committed to SBIC	$2.6 million	$2.8 million	Yes	
SBA	SBIC		Cost per small business assisted	None	$19,645	N/A	
SBA	New Markets Venture Capital (NMVC) Program The purpose of the NMVC program is to promote economic development and the creation of wealth and job opportunities in low-income geographic areas and among individuals living in such areas through developmental venture capital investments in smaller enterprises located in such areas. Through public-private partnerships between SBA and businesses, the program is designed to serve the unmet equity needs of local entrepreneurs through developmental venture capital investments, provide technical assistance to small businesses, create quality employment opportunities for low-income area residents, and build wealth within low-income areas.	$0[m]	Eligible small businesses assisted	None	N/A	N/A	N/A

GAO-12-819 Entrepreneurial Assistance

Agency	Program Name and Mission	Fiscal year 2011 Obligations[a]	Performance Measures	Fiscal year 2011 Performance Goal	Fiscal year 2011 Actual Performance[b]	Met Individual Goals	Met All Goals
SBA	Federal and State Technology Partnership (FAST) Program	$1,885,096	Eligible small businesses assisted	None	N/A	N/A	N/A
	The purpose of the FAST program is to strengthen the technological competitiveness of small business concerns in the U.S. by improving the participation of small technology firms in the innovation and commercialization of new technology.						
SBA	FAST		Outreach events held	None	N/A	N/A	
SBA	International Trade	$7,681,000	Loans approved	$400 million	$924 million	Yes	Yes
	The International Trade program helps small business exporters by providing loans for a number of activities specifically designed to help them develop or expand their export activities.						
SBA	International Trade		Small and medium sized exporters assisted	990	1,346	Yes	
SBA	International Trade		Lenders counseled/trained	4,000	6,790	Yes	
SBA	International Trade		Cost per small and medium sized exporter assisted	None	$5,707	N/A	
U.S. Department of Agriculture (USDA)	Intermediary Relending Program	$7,364,000	Jobs created and saved	14,600	14,601	Yes	Yes
	The purpose of the program is to alleviate poverty and increase economic activity and employment in rural communities. Under the program, loans are provided to local organizations (intermediaries) for the establishment of revolving loan funds. These revolving loan funds are used to assist with financing business and economic development activity to create or retain jobs in disadvantaged and remote communities.						
USDA	Rural Business Enterprise Grants Program	$ 38,586,000	Jobs created or saved	14,330	13,265	No	No
	The program provides grants for rural projects that finance and facilitate development of small and emerging rural						

GAO-12-819 Entrepreneurial Assistance

Agency	Program Name and Mission	Fiscal year 2011 Obligations[a]	Performance Measures	Fiscal year 2011 Performance Goal	Fiscal year 2011 Actual Performance[b]	Met Individual Goals	Met All Goals
	businesses, help fund business incubators, and help fund employment-related adult education programs. To assist with business development, the program may fund a broad array of activities.						
USDA	Rural Business Opportunity Grant Program The program promotes sustainable economic development in rural communities with exceptional needs through provision of training and technical assistance for business development, entrepreneurs, and economic development officials and to assist with economic development planning.	$2,581,000	Businesses assisted	950	586	No	No
USDA	Rural Microentrepreneur Assistance Program The purpose of the program is to support the development and ongoing success of rural microentrepreneurs and microenterprises. Direct loans and grants are made to selected microenterprise development organizations.	$6,668,000	Jobs created or saved	580	1240	Yes	Yes
USDA	Rural Cooperative Development Grants The primary objective of this grant program is to improve the economic condition of rural areas through the creation or retention of jobs and development of new rural cooperatives, value-added processing, and other rural businesses. Grant funds are provided for the establishment and operation of centers that have the expertise or that can contract out for the expertise to assist individuals or entities in the start-up, expansion, or operational improvement of rural businesses, especially cooperative or mutually owned businesses.	$8,424,000	Businesses assisted	326	324	No	No

Appendix III: Performance Goals and Accomplishments for 52 Programs that Can Support Entrepreneurs, Fiscal Year 2011

Agency	Program Name and Mission	Fiscal year 2011 Obligations[a]	Performance Measures	Fiscal year 2011 Performance Goal	Fiscal year 2011 Actual Performance[b]	Met Individual Goals	Met All Goals
USDA	Business and Industry Guaranteed Loans The purpose of the program is to improve, develop, or finance business, industry, and employment and improve the economic and environmental climate in rural communities. This purpose is achieved by bolstering the existing private credit structure through the guarantee of quality loans.	$70,202,000	Jobs created or saved	11,705	27,806	Yes	Yes
USDA	Value Added Producer Grants The purpose of this program is to assist eligible independent agricultural commodity producers, agriculture producer groups, farmer and rancher cooperatives, and majority-controlled producer-based businesses in developing strategies and business plans to further refine or enhance their products, thereby increasing their value to end users and increasing returns to producers.	$1,318,000	Businesses assisted	151	0	No	No
USDA	Small Socially-Disadvantaged Producer Grants The primary objective of the program is to provide technical assistance to small, socially disadvantaged agricultural producers through eligible cooperatives and associations of cooperatives. Grants are awarded on a competitive basis.	$2,940,000	None	None	N/A	N/A	N/A
USDA	1890 Land Grant Institutions Rural Entrepreneurial Outreach Program/Rural Business Entrepreneur Development Initiative[n] The purposes of this program are to encourage 1890 Institutions to provide technical assistance for business creation in economically challenged rural communities, to conduct educational programs that develop and improve	$0	None	None	N/A	N/A	N/A

GAO-12-819 Entrepreneurial Assistance

Agency	Program Name and Mission	Fiscal year 2011 Obligations[a]	Performance Measures	Fiscal year 2011 Performance Goal	Fiscal year 2011 Actual Performance[b]	Met Individual Goals	Met All Goals
	upon the professional skills of rural entrepreneurs, and to provide outreach and promote USDA Rural Development programs in small rural communities with the greatest economic need.						
USDA	Agriculture Innovation Center Award grants to centers around the country to provide technical and business development assistance to agricultural producers seeking to enter into ventures that add value to commodities or products they produce.	$0	None	N/A	N/A	N/A	N/A
USDA	Small Business Innovation Research This program aims to stimulate technological innovation in the private sector; strengthen the role of small businesses in meeting federal research and development needs; increase private-sector commercialization of innovations derived from USDA-supported research and development efforts; and foster and encourage participation by women-owned and socially disadvantaged small business firms in technological innovation.	$22,635,200	Percentage of Phase 2 businesses that have achieved commercial success, as a result of increased sales	50%	Data collection ongoing because performance data are collected over a 2-year time period.	Not available	Not available
USDA	Biomass Research and Development Initiative Competitive Grants Program This program awards grants to support the research and development and demonstration of biofuels and biobased products. It is a joint effort between USDA and the U.S. Department of Energy.	$2,075,000	Number of technologies successfully deployed	None	N/A	N/A	N/A

Agency	Program Name and Mission	Fiscal year 2011 Obligations[a]	Performance Measures	Fiscal year 2011 Performance Goal	Fiscal year 2011 Actual Performance[b]	Met Individual Goals	Met All Goals
USDA	Woody Biomass Utilization Grant Program This program provides financial grants to businesses and communities that use woody biomass removed from National Forest System hazardous fuel reduction projects. Grants are awarded on a competitive basis.	$3,000,000	Green tons of woody biomass removed and used	None	N/A	N/A	N/A

Source: GAO analysis of information provided by Commerce, HUD, SBA, and USDA.

Notes:

[a]Fiscal year 2011 obligations were provided by agency officials for each program. HUD's figures represent fiscal year 2011 actual budget authority rather than obligations. SBA figures represent fiscal year 2011 fully allocated costs rather than obligations.

[b]While some programs listed in the table did not set fiscal year 2011 performance goals, most of the programs that had goals reported actual performance that could be compared with these goals.

[c]EDA does not collect performance information (i.e., jobs created and private investment) by program, rather this information is aggregated for all EDA programs.

[d]Commerce's Native American Business Enterprise Centers program incurred obligations in fiscal year 2011, but Commerce officials could not provide funding data at the program level. Funding for this program is included in the fiscal year 2011 obligations for Commerce's Minority Business Center program. Similarly, Commerce could not provide performance measure data at the program level because it tracks its activity as part of the Minority Business Center program.

[e]This figure is an estimate of actual budget authority used for activities that GAO categorizes as economic development, rather than total program expenditures, and does not include other costs for activities such as housing or public services.

[f]This figure is an estimate of actual budget authority used for activities that GAO categorizes as economic development, rather than total program expenditures, and does not include other costs for activities such as housing or public services.

[g]This figure is an estimate of actual budget authority used for activities that GAO categorizes as economic development, rather than total program expenditures, and does not include other costs for activities such as housing or public services.

[h]This figure is an estimate of actual budget authority used for activities that GAO categorizes as economic development, rather than total program expenditures, and does not include other costs for activities such as housing or public services.

[i]According to HUD officials, the performance measures for the CDBG Disaster Recovery Grant program can vary and they did not provide us any set fiscal year 2011 goals.

[j]HUD officials stated that the Rural Innovation Fund program is new and they are in the process of establishing goals.

[k]HUD officials noted that $31,355,236 in 5-year grants was awarded in September, 2011 through this program, but they will not be obligated until after FY 2011. These funds include $25,000,000 that was appropriated in FY 2010 for the program and additional funds recaptured through HUD's Rural Housing and Economic Development program.

[l]The performance goal and actual figures for this performance measure are for the two-year period consisting of FY 2010 and FY 2011. SBA officials indicated that a goal was not set for FY 2011 alone.

[m]According to SBA officials, the New Markets Venture Capital program is a one-time pilot program that received one-time funding in fiscal year 2001.

[n]USDA's 1890 program does not have a congressional appropriation but is instead funded through USDA's Salaries and Expenses account. Funding is not reported separately for this program and is listed as $0 here, but this is an active and funded program.

Appendix IV: Additional Federal Programs that Can Fund Economic Activities

We reviewed the 2011 *Catalog of Federal Domestic Assistance* (CFDA) and identified 95 additional federal programs that can support at least one of the nine economic activities identified in appendix II (see table 3). These programs, while not comprehensive, are in addition to the 80 economic development programs administered by Commerce, HUD, SBA, and USDA that we included in previous reports. We identified these 94 programs based on our comparison of CFDA program descriptions with the nine economic activities as illustrated in appendix II. However, others conducting similar analyses may come to different conclusions on which federal programs support economic development. Additionally, 32 of the 64 federal agencies and departments listed in the CFDA did not provide descriptions for their programs within the 2011 CFDA, which prevented us from assessing whether those programs are related to economic development. Many of the agencies that administer these additional programs have missions that do not directly focus on economic development. For example, a number of the programs listed for the Department of Health and Human Services focus on health-related research, but also participate in at least one of the economic development activities we have identified.

Table 3: Additional Federal Programs That Can Fund Economic Activities, as Listed in the 2011 Catalog of Federal Domestic Assistance

Agency	Name	Program number	Economic activities								
			Strategic planning & research	Commercial buildings	Business incubators & accelerators	Industrial parks & buildings	Physical infrastructure	Entrepreneurial efforts	Marketing & new markets	Telecommunications & broadband infrastructure	Tourism
Appalachian Regional Commission	Appalachian Regional Development	23.001	X		X	X	X	X	X	X	X
Appalachian Regional Commission	Appalachian Area Development	23.002	X		X	X		X	X	X	X
Appalachian Regional Commission	Appalachian Development Highway System	23.003					X				
Appalachian Regional Commission	Appalachian Local Development District Assistance	23.009	X								
Appalachian Regional Commission	Appalachian Research, Technical Assistance, and Demonstration Projects	23.011	X								
Denali Commission	Denali Commission Program	90.100					X				
Department of Defense	Community Economic Adjustment	12.600	X								
Department of Energy	Nuclear Energy Research, Development and Demonstration	81.121						X			
Department of Energy	Granting Of Patent Licenses	81.003						X	X		
Department of Energy	Inventions and Innovations	81.036						X			

Appendix IV: Additional Federal Programs
that Can Fund Economic Activities

Agency	Name	Program number	Economic activities								
			Strategic planning & research	Commercial buildings	Business incubators & accelerators	Industrial parks & buildings	Physical infrastructure	Entrepreneurial efforts	Marketing & new markets	Telecommunications & broadband infrastructure	Tourism
Department of Energy	State Energy Program	81.041					X				
Department of Energy	Federal Loan Guarantees for Innovative Energy Technologies	81.126			X		X	X	X		
Department of Health and Human Services	Indian Health Service Sanitation Facilities Construction Program	93.445					X				
Department of Health and Human Services	Cancer Control	93.399						X			
Department of Health and Human Services	Consumer Operated and Oriented Plan [CO-OP] Program	93.545						X			
Department of Health and Human Services	Community Services Block Grant Discretionary Awards	93.570	X	X	X		X	X	X		
Department of Health and Human Services	Refugee and Entrant Assistance Discretionary Grants	93.576						X	X		
Department of Health and Human Services	Job Opportunities for Low-Income Individuals	93.593	X					X			

GAO-12-819 Entrepreneurial Assistance

Agency	Name	Program number	Economic activities								
			Strategic planning & research	Commercial buildings	Business incubators & accelerators	Industrial parks & buildings	Physical infrastructure	Entrepreneurial efforts	Marketing & new markets	Telecommunications & broadband infrastructure	Tourism
Department of Health and Human Services	Assets for Independence Demonstration Program	93.602						X			
Department of Health and Human Services	Native American Programs	93.612	X	X[a]	X	X[a]	X[a]	X	X	X	X
Department of Health and Human Services	Cardiovascular Diseases Research	93.837						X			
Department of Health and Human Services	Lung Diseases Research	93.838						X			
Department of Health and Human Services	Blood Diseases and Resources Research	93.839						X			
Department of Health and Human Services	Arthritis, Musculoskeletal and Skin Diseases Research	93.846						X			
Department of Health and Human Services	Diabetes, Digestive, and Kidney Diseases Extramural Research	93.847						X			
Department of Health and Human Services	Extramural Research Programs in the Neurosciences and Neurological Disorders	93.853						X			

Agency	Name	Program number	Economic activities								
			Strategic planning & research	Commercial buildings	Business incubators & accelerators	Industrial parks & buildings	Physical infrastructure	Entrepreneurial efforts	Marketing & new markets	Telecommuni-cations & broadband infrastructure	Tourism
Department of Health and Human Services	Allergy, Immunology and Transplantation Research	93.855						X			
Department of Health and Human Services	Child Health and Human Development Extramural Research	93.865						X			
Department of Health and Human Services	Aging Research	93.866						X			
Department of Health and Human Services	Vision Research	93.867						X			
Department of Health and Human Services	Medical Library Assistance	93.879						X			
Department of Homeland Security	Operation Safe Commerce Cooperative Agreement Program	97.058						X			
Department of Labor	Workforce Investment Act—Adult Program	17.258						X			
Department of Labor	Workforce Investment Act—Dislocated Workers	17.260						X			
Department of the Interior	National Heritage Area Federal Financial Assistance	15.939	X	X		X	X	X	X		X

GAO-12-819 Entrepreneurial Assistance

Agency	Name	Program number	Economic activities								
			Strategic planning & research	Commercial buildings	Business incubators & accelerators	Industrial parks & buildings	Physical infrastructure	Entrepreneurial efforts	Marketing & new markets	Telecommunications & broadband infrastructure	Tourism
Department of the Interior	Tribal Self-Governance	15.022					X				
Department of the Interior	Road Maintenance Indian Roads	15.033					X				
Department of the Interior	Minerals and Mining on Indian Lands	15.038						X			
Department of the Interior	Indian Loans Economic Development	15.124						X			
Department of the Interior	National Fire Plan - Wildland Urban Interface Community Fire Assistance	15.228						X			
Department of the Interior	Water Reclamation and Reuse Program	15.504					X				
Department of the Interior	WaterSMART (Sustain and Manage America's Resources for Tomorrow)	15.507					X				
Department of the Interior	Colorado River Basin Salinity Control Program	15.509					X				
Department of the Interior	Colorado Ute Indian Water Rights Settlement Act	15.510					X				
Department of the Interior	Fort Peck Reservation Rural Water System	15.516					X				

Agency	Name	Program number	Economic activities								
			Strategic planning & research	Commercial buildings	Business incubators & accelerators	Industrial parks & buildings	Physical infrastructure	Entrepreneurial efforts	Marketing & new markets	Telecommunications & broadband infrastructure	Tourism
Department of the Interior	Garrison Diversion Unit	15.518					X				
Department of the Interior	Indian Tribal Water Resources Development, Management, and Protection	15.519					X				
Department of the Interior	Lewis and Clark Rural Water System	15.520					X				
Department of the Interior	Mni Wiconi Rural Water Supply Project	15.522					X				
Department of the Interior	Perkins County Rural Water System	15.523					X				
Department of the Interior	Rocky Boy's/North Central Montana Regional Water System	15.525					X				
Department of the Interior	San Gabriel Basin Restoration Project	15.526					X				
Department of the Interior	Yakima River Basin Water Enhancement Project	15.531					X				
Department of the Interior	Colorado River Basin Projects Act of 1968	15.541					X				
Department of the Interior	Lower Colorado River Multi-species Conservation Project	15.538					X				

GAO-12-819 Entrepreneurial Assistance

Agency	Name	Program number	Economic activities								
			Strategic planning & research	Commercial buildings	Business incubators & accelerators	Industrial parks & buildings	Physical infrastructure	Entrepreneurial efforts	Marketing & new markets	Telecommunications & broadband infrastructure	Tourism
Department of the Interior	Navajo-Gallup Water Supply Project	15.552					X				
Department of the Interior	Economic, Social, and Political Development of the Territories	15.875		X	X	X	X	X		X	
Department of the Interior	Historic Preservation Fund Grants-In-Aid	15.904	X	X	X		X	X			X
Department of the Interior	Preservation of Historic Structures on the Campuses of Historically Black Colleges and Universities	15.932	X		X		X	X			X
Department of the Interior	Preservation of Japanese American Confinement Sites	15.933	X	X							X
Department of the Treasury	Native Initiatives	21.012						X			
Department of the Treasury	Community Development Financial Institutions Program	21.020						X			
Department of the Treasury	Bank Enterprise Award Program	21.021						X			
Department of Transportation	Airport Improvement Program	20.106					X				

Agency	Name	Program number	Economic activities								
			Strategic planning & research	Commercial buildings	Business incubators & accelerators	Industrial parks & buildings	Physical infrastructure	Entrepreneurial efforts	Marketing & new markets	Telecommunications & broadband infrastructure	Tourism
Department of Transportation	Highway Planning and Construction	20.205					X				
Department of Transportation	Transportation Infrastructure Finance and Innovation Act Program	20.223					X				
Department of Transportation	Railroad Development	20.314					X				
Department of Transportation	National Railroad Passenger Corporation Grants	20.315					X				
Department of Transportation	Railroad Rehabilitation and Improvement Financing Program	20.316		X		X	X	X			
Department of Transportation	Capital Assistance to States-Intercity Passenger Rail Service	20.317					X				
Department of Transportation	Maglev Project Selection Program-Safetea-Lu	20.318					X				
Department of Transportation	High-Speed Rail Corridors and Intercity Passenger Rail Service Capital Assistance Grants	20.319					X				

Agency	Name	Program number	Economic activities								
			Strategic planning & research	Commercial buildings	Business incubators & accelerators	Industrial parks & buildings	Physical infrastructure	Entrepreneurial efforts	Marketing & new markets	Telecommunications & broadband infrastructure	Tourism
Department of Transportation	Rail Line Relocation and Improvement	20.320					X				
Department of Transportation	Federal Transit Capital Investment Grants	20.500					X				
Department of Transportation	Paul S. Sarbanes Transit in the Parks	20.520					X				
Department of Transportation	Federal Ship Financing Guarantees	20.802					X	X			
Department of Transportation	Assistance to Small Shipyards	20.814					X	X			
Department of Transportation	America's Marine Highway Grants	20.816					X				
Department of Transportation	Bonding Assistance Program	20.904						X			
Department of Transportation	Disadvantaged Business Enterprises Short Term Lending Program	20.905						X			
Department of Transportation	Assistance to Small and Disadvantaged Businesses	20.910						X			
Department of Transportation	Payments for Small Community Air Service Development	20.930							X		X
Department of Transportation	National Infrastructure Investments	20.933					X				

Appendix IV: Additional Federal Programs that Can Fund Economic Activities

			Economic activities								
Agency	Name	Program number	Strategic planning & research	Commercial buildings	Business incubators & accelerators	Industrial parks & buildings	Physical infrastructure	Entrepreneurial efforts	Marketing & new markets	Telecommunications & broadband infrastructure	Tourism
Environmental Protection Agency	Healthy Communities Grant Program	66.110					X				X
Environmental Protection Agency	Environmental Finance Center Grants	66.203					X				
Environmental Protection Agency	Construction Grants for Wastewater Treatment Works	66.418					X				
Environmental Protection Agency	Capitalization Grants for Clean Water State Revolving Funds	66.458					X				
Environmental Protection Agency	Capitalization Grants for Drinking Water State Revolving Funds	66.468					X				
Environmental Protection Agency	Environmental Justice Small Grant Program	66.604	X								
Environmental Protection Agency	Pollution Prevention Grants Program	66.708						X			
National Endowment for the Humanities	Challenge Grants	45.130					X				
National Endowment for the Humanities	Promotion of the Humanities Public Programs	45.164									X
National Endowment for the Humanities	Digital Humanities Start-up Grants	45.169						X			

**Appendix IV: Additional Federal Programs
that Can Fund Economic Activities**

					Economic activities						
Agency	Name	Program number	Strategic planning & research	Commercial buildings	Business incubators & accelerators	Industrial parks & buildings	Physical infrastructure	Entrepreneurial efforts	Marketing & new markets	Telecommunications & broadband infrastructure	Tourism
National Science Foundation	Engineering Grants	47.041						X			

Source: GAO analysis of the Catalog of Federal Domestic Assistance (2011 edition).

[a]The authority of Health and Human Service's Native American program is limited regarding construction. Its authority is limited to minor construction activities and does not allow for the building of structures from the ground up or other major construction activities.

Author(s), title of evaluation	Agency reviewed	Program(s) reviewed	Purpose of the study	Data and methods used
Grant Thornton, *Construction Grants Program Impact Assessment Report*, September 2008	Department of Commerce (Commerce) – Economic Development Administration (EDA)	Grants for Public Works and Economic Development Facilities Economic Adjustment Assistance	To assess the economic impacts and federal costs of EDA's construction program, and to improve upon EDA's prior study in 1997 in terms of using a more robust regression model.	Data for this study were taken from EDA's Operations and Planning and Control System for construction projects' status and funding between fiscal years 1990-2005 and Bureau of Labor Statistics county employment data. Study used ordinary and two-stage least squares regression.
Beth Walter Honadle and Michael C. Carroll, Center for Policy Analysis & Public Service, Bowling Green State University, *Local Technical Assistance Program Evaluation*, 2003	Commerce EDA	Economic Development– Technical Assistance	To evaluate the local Technical Assistance program for fiscal years 1997 and 1998 to determine the extent to which the program has achieved its mission of helping communities solve specific problems, respond to economic development opportunities, and build and expand organizational capacity in distressed areas.	The evaluation is based on data collected from • project files and data obtained from EDA headquarters and six regional offices, • surveys of 121 grant recipients, and • two on-site case studies in each EDA region.
Mt. Auburn Associates, Inc., *An Evaluation of EDA's University Center Program*, December 2001	Commerce EDA	Economic Development– Technical Assistance	To evaluate the University Center Program in five areas: • effectiveness in meeting economic development needs, • effectiveness in targeting distressed areas, • distribution of centers being optimal under EDA budget constraints, • duplication or overlap with other federal programs, and • leveraging resources.	Study collected data from numerous sources: • interviews with EDA national and regional staff, • compilation of a database on University Center characteristics and activities from documents such as grant applications, • interviews with Center directors, • Center client survey, and • site visits.
Wayne State University, *Evaluation of EDA's Planning Program: Economic Development Districts*, May 2002	Commerce EDA	Economic Development– Support for Planning Organizations	To evaluate the overall impact of EDA's Economic Development District (EDD) Planning program, which funds the EDDs; highlight commonalities and differences among the various EDDs; as well as to assess if the program promotes regional cooperation towards making an impact on the economic development goals of the community.	Data were gathered in several progressive stages: • site visits, • general survey, • additional site visits, and • a second survey to respondents of first survey. Analysis of these data was done using statistical techniques such as principle-component analysis.

Author(s), title of evaluation	Agency reviewed	Program(s) reviewed	Purpose of the study	Data and methods used
The Urban Institute, *The Impact of CDBG Spending on Urban Neighborhoods*, October 2002	Department of Housing and Urban Development (HUD)	Community Development Block Grant (CDBG)/Entitlement Grants	• To find indicators for the effect of CDBG spending and track changes in these indicators. • To report on neighborhoods that had received a large amount of CDBG funding.	• Classified cities into two categories: those that had available data that were more detailed and those that had less-detailed available data • Identify CDBG investment levels that must be complemented with additional investment to produce significant improvements in neighborhood outcomes.
The Urban Institute, *Public-Sector Loans to Private-Sector Businesses: An Assessment of HUD-Supported Local Economic Development Lending Activities*, December 2002	HUD	CDBG/Entitlement Grants CDBG/States CDBG/Section 108 Loan Guarantees CDBG/Brownfields Economic Development Initiative (BEDI)	• To determine the results of local third-party lending programs in terms of business development and job creation benefits. • To determine whether some kinds of borrowers in certain types of neighborhoods create jobs or leverage private funds at lower cost than others.	Study was based on • telephone interviews with Economic Development directors in 460 of the 972 entitlement communities that used CDBG funds, and interviews with 234 of the 750 business borrowers. • sample of business loans to those areas, matched with Dun and Bradstreet information. Study examines various indicators of program performance, including • business survival rates, • rates of total and low-income job creation, • retention relative to jobs planned at the time of loan origination, • public costs of each job created, • amount of private funding induced (or leveraged) by program loans, and • rates at which public loan dollars substitute for private funds that would have otherwise been invested.
Econometrica, Inc, *Evaluation of the Indian Community Block Grant Program*, May 2006	HUD	CDBG/Indian	To measure the outcomes of Indian CDBG expenditures. The outcomes included amount of leveraged funding obtained by grantees, enhancements of partnering relationships, and level of economic activity in the communities.	Study had three main data sources: (1) grant file reviews of program data, (2) telephone survey of grant participants, and (3) case study observations.

Author(s), title of evaluation	Agency reviewed	Program(s) reviewed	Purpose of the study	Data and methods used
Social Compact and Weinheimer & Associates, *Assessing Section 4: Helping CDC's to Grow and Serve*, February 2011	HUD	Section 4 Capacity Building for Affordable Housing and Community Development	To evaluate the effect of the Section 4 program on improving organization capacity. The section 4 program was set up to support training for Community Development Corporations (CDC) and to help CDCs grow and serve.	From 2001 through 2009, data were collected from (1) interviews of key staff at intermediaries, (2) online survey of 360 CDCs that received Section 4 grants, and (3) interviews with leaders of 34 Section 4-asssisted CDCs.
Concentrance Consulting Group, *Impact Study of Entrepreneurial Development Resources*, 2002 – 2010[a]	Small Business Administration (SBA)	Small Business Development Centers Women's Business Centers SCORE	To assess the impact of SBA's entrepreneurial development programs on small businesses, including businesses' perceptions of the programs and their economic growth as a result of the services provided.	Study included survey of clients served by SBA's entrepreneurial businesses. Sample size approximately 6,500 observations across all years–2007, 2008 and 2010 with a smaller sample in 2007.
Gwen Richtermeyer and Karen Fife-Samyn, Quality Research Associates, *Analyzing the Impact of the Women's Business Center Program*, July 2004.	SBA	Women's Business Centers	To analyze the economic impact of the SBA's Women's Business Center program. Specifically the study addressed the following between 2001 and 2003: • impact on growth of firms • factors that account for success • specific program model that predicts success • predictors of positive economic outcomes, and • effect of client demographics on outcomes.	Study includes a set of descriptive statistics on the rate of growth in the number of Women's Business Center clients and also the rate of jobs and profits at those centers. Study used a regression to test the association between clients and other outcomes.
Mary Godwyn, Nan Langowitz, and Norean Sharpe, Center for Women's Leadership at Babson College, *The Impact and Influence of Women's Business Centers in the United States*, April 2005	SBA	Women's Business Centers	To examine the economic impact and effectiveness of Women's Business Centers.	Survey and focus group of 100 Women's Business Centers.
The Urban Institute, *A Performance Analysis of SBA's Loan and Investment Programs*, January 2008	SBA	7(a) Loan Program 504 Loan Program Small Business Investment Company (SBIC) Program	In order to test whether SBA loan guarantees are associated with positive firm outcomes, this study addressed the following questions: • What happens to sales, employment and survival before and after firms receive the guarantee? • What explains the changes observed?	SBA administrative data were obtained on firms participating in 7(a), 504 or SBIC programs. For these firms, data were obtained from Dun and Bradstreet on firm outcomes. The study used a multivariate statistical technique to estimate whether (a) the change in outcome was significant, and (b) whether

Author(s), title of evaluation	Agency reviewed	Program(s) reviewed	Purpose of the study	Data and methods used
				other factors (such as business type) affect the change in outcome.
The Urban Institute, *An Assessment of Small Business Administration Loan and Investment Performance: Survey of Assisted Businesses*, January 2008	SBA	7(a) Loan Program 504 Loan Program Microloan Program SBIC	To produce a survey that is intended provide customer satisfaction indicators for the 7(a), 504, SBIC, and MicroLoan programs.	Beginning from a sample of assisted firms from Dunn and Bradstreet, a survey was sent to approximately 3,000 firms. The surveyed firms had received the loans 6 or 7 years prior to the questionnaire.
Henry Beale and Nicola Deas, Microeconomic Applications, Inc., *The HUBZone Program Report*, May 2008[b]	SBA	HUBZone (Historically Underutilized Business Zone)	To examine the effectiveness of the HUBZone program.	Data are from three databases: applications for HUBZone certification, Central Contractor Registration on small businesses, and the Federal Procurement Data System for information on HUBZone businesses that have won HUBZone contracts. The report primarily used an input-output approach to estimate the impact on the HUBZone areas. In this approach, direct and indirect impacts are measured using the above three databases and multipliers from Bureau of Economic Analysis.
Charles W. Wessner, Editor, Committee on Capitalizing on Science, Technology, and Innovation, *An Assessment of the Small Business Innovation Research Program at the National Science Foundation*, 2008.	SBA	Small Business Innovation Research Program (SBIR)	The study attempts to determine the effectiveness of the SBIR program in • stimulating technological innovation; • using small businesses to meet federal needs; • increasing private sector commercialization; and • encouraging participation of minority and other disadvantaged groups.	Study is based on National Research Council surveys and reviews of agency materials. Study includes surveys and also case studies.

Author(s), title of evaluation	Agency reviewed	Program(s) reviewed	Purpose of the study	Data and methods used
M.A. Boland, J.C. Crespi, and D. Oswald, *How Successful Was the 2002 Farm Bill's Value-Added Producer Grant Program?*, December 2007	Department of Agriculture (USDA)	Value Added Producer Grants (VAPG)	To identify the determinants for success among USDA's VAPG.	Survey of 739 VAPG recipients, out of which 621 responded. A statistical analysis was conducted using binary logistical regression (logit) and cumulative logit models.

Source: GAO analysis of information provided by Commerce, HUD, SBA and USDA.

[a]While SBA conducts annual impact surveys of the SBDC, WBC, and SCORE programs, for purposes of this report we focused on the most recent impact study conducted of these programs.

[b]In a previous GAO report, Small Business Administration: Additional Actions Are Needed to Certify and Monitor HUBZone Businesses and Assess Program Results, GAO-08-643 (Washington, D.C.: Jun. 17, 2008), we recommended that SBA further develop measures and implement plans to assess the effectiveness of the HUBZone program. SBA took steps to conduct such an assessment. However, SBA has since decided to rely on the 2008 study conducted by SBA's Office of Advocacy listed in this appendix.

United States Department of Agriculture
Rural Development
Office of the Under Secretary

AUG - 1 2012

Mr. William Shear
Director, Financial Markets and Community Investment
Government Accountability Office
441 G Street, NW
Washington, D.C. 20548

Dear Mr. Shear:

U.S. Department of Agriculture (USDA) would like to thank you for the opportunity to comment on the Government Accountability Office's (GAO) Draft Report entitled, "Entrepreneurial Assistance: Opportunities Exist to Improve Programs' Collaboration, Data-Tracking, and Performance Management" (GAO 12-819).

USDA agrees with GAO that entrepreneurs play a vital role in the U.S. economy. USDA also agrees with GAO that no duplication exist among Federal programs that assist entrepreneurs.

USDA, Rural Development (RD) mission area respectfully disagrees with some of the comments and observations made in the report.

First, the report broadly portrays Federal programs that assist entrepreneurs and does not highlight the unique characteristics of each agency. Listed below are some of the ways RD's Rural Business-Cooperative Service (RBS) agency helps rural communities create wealth so they become self-sustaining, repopulating, and economically thriving:

1. RBS specializes in rural economic development.
2. RBS delivers its programs and services through a network of 47 RD State Offices and local area offices located in rural communities throughout the United States.

1400 Independence Ave., S.W. • Washington, DC 20250-0700
Web: http://www.rurdev.usda.gov

Committed to the future of rural communities

"USDA is an equal opportunity provider, employer and lender."
To file a complaint of discrimination write USDA, Director, Office of Civil Rights,
1400 Independence Avenue, S.W., Washington, DC 20250-9410 or call (800) 795-3272 (Voice) or (202) 720-6382 (TDD).

Mr. William Shear   2

3. RBS provides guidance and services that help entrepreneurs achieve their business goals, repay their loans, and create jobs in rural communities.
4. RBS offers a holistic portfolio of grant, loan, and grant/loan combination programs to assist rural entrepreneurs of all levels from start-up to commercialization.
5. RBS provides financing and training options to rural businesses.

Second, GAO highlights examples where entrepreneurs may be eligible for multiple federal programs based on an entrepreneur's specific characteristics. However, the report does not mention if this is a pervasive or problematic issue. It is RBS' experience that rural entrepreneurs may be eligible for multiple programs, and a businesses' unique situation dictates which programs best meet its needs.

For example, the loan limits and terms vary between RBS' Business and Industry Guaranteed Loan Program (B&I) and the Small Business Administration's (SBA) 7(a) Loan Program. Each entrepreneur must work with its lender to identify the program that best meets its specific borrowing needs. In these instances, the RBS and SBA programs complement each other and serve a larger number of entrepreneurs.

RBS continuously seeks opportunities to encourage increased investment in rural economic development through collaboration and leveraging. In a recent survey of 41 RD State Offices, 100 percent of those surveyed said they promote SBA programs with their resource partners, such as lenders. In Fiscal Year (FY) 2011, the RBS Administrator emphasized leveraging B&I program dollars with "other funds" to increase funding for projects. Additionally, the FY 2011 Business and Cooperative Programs Goals letter required each RD State Office to leverage at least 40 percent of their obligated funds.

Rural communities have historically lacked adequate access to private investment capital to support business development and job creation. In 2011 and 2012, RD and SBA collaborated to host six roundtable discussions on increasing private investment capital for rural small businesses. The partnership stems from RBS' research into capital markets. Representatives from the financial industry, Farm Credit Administration, and State agencies participated at these meetings. RBS will continue to work with other Federal agencies to ensure that rural communities are economically thriving.

Third, in reference to GAO's comments on data-collecting process, RBS uses the following tools to identify and improve the effectiveness of its programs:

1. RBS gathers data on all its programs and projects, which it analyzes to assess program effectiveness.
2. RBS maintains the data in an electronic database as well as project files.
3. RBS regularly evaluates all of its programs at the National and State levels.
4. RBS uses RD's Management Control Review (MCR) process to assess a program's effectiveness.

Mr. William Shear   3

5. RBS uses its Business and Cooperative Program Assessment Review (BCPAR) process
    to determine each RD State Office's effectiveness in administering the Agency's
    programs.

Finally, the recommendations in the report are not explicit, which makes it unclear how RBS
would effectively address each recommendation to GAO's satisfaction.

In conclusion, USDA RD is committed to expanding economic opportunities for all
entrepreneurs. We appreciate any information that helps the Federal Government efficiency
and effectively deliver its programs and services. These internal assessments are particularly
important as we seek new opportunities to direct funding to programs and reduce our
administrative costs.

Again, thank you for the opportunity to comment on the report. If you have any questions,
please contact John Purcell, Director, Financial Management Division, at (202) 692-0080.

Sincerely,

Dallas Tonsager
Under Secretary

Appendix VII: Comments from the Department of Commerce

UNITED STATES DEPARTMENT OF COMMERCE
The Secretary of Commerce
Washington, D.C. 20230

August 6, 2012

Mr. William B. Shear
Director, Financial Markets and
  Community Investment
U.S. Government Accountability Office
441 G Street NW
Washington, DC 20548

Dear Mr. Shear:

The Department of Commerce appreciates the opportunity to review and comment on the U.S. Government Accountability Office (GAO) draft report entitled, *Entrepreneurial Assistance: Opportunities Exist To Improve Programs' Collaboration, Data-Tracking, and Performance Management* (GAO-12-819). Our comments are enclosed.

Thank you for your work on this report. If you have any questions, please contact me or Jim Stowers, Acting Assistant Secretary for Legislative and Intergovernmental Affairs, at (202) 482-3663.

Sincerely,

Rebecca M. Blank
Acting Secretary of Commerce

Enclosure

**Department of Commerce
Economic Development Administration
Comments on Draft GAO Report Entitled**
*Entrepreneurial Assistance: Opportunities Exist to Improve
Programs' Collaboration, Data-Tracking, and Performance Management*
(GAO-12-819)

The U.S. Department of Commerce provides the following comments:

Native American Business Enterprise Centers

A footnote should be added to the performance measures data associated with the Native
American Business Enterprise Centers (NABEC) program on page 41, and all entries
revised to zero. The footnote should indicate that performance for the NABEC is part of
the performance of the Minority Business Center program on the next page. This would
be comparable to the existing footnote regarding funding for the NABEC program, which
is also entered as a zero.

Entrepreneurial Assistance

As previously stated by EDA, every federal agency shares some degree of commonality
regarding their missions, their administration, and their outputs. This provides agencies
with the opportunity to improve operational efficiency by identifying best practices
across government. Further, it enables agencies to better define their respective goals and
objectives relative to each other. Most importantly, this commonality recognizes that
services meet a continuum of needs along more than one dimension. Thus, what may
appear as duplication at a higher level is in reality a portfolio of distinct services meeting
unique needs. However, GAO may wish to consider the complementary role many
agencies play in the field of economic development – and the need for such varied, but
complementary, activities to specifically address the complexities of entrepreneurs.

Entrepreneurship is not a singular activity, but is the sum of multiple unique activities
that start with an idea, and finishes with commercialization – the sale of products and
services to the public. The report is silent on both the varied needs of entrepreneurs in
communities across the country and on the specific outcomes, activities, and services the
existing federal entrepreneurial programs are directed towards. Not all entrepreneurs (or
the communities in which they reside) require the same set of services. EDA has carved a
niche, for example, in supporting cluster development, regional innovation ecosystems,
and many of the associated infrastructure needs, which is a unique characteristic among
federal agencies engaged in economic development -- and just one of many needs of
entrepreneurs.

In addition, it is important to acknowledge the underlying forces which guide the
uniqueness of federal agencies' responses to entrepreneurial assistance, including, in

many cases, unique eligibility requirements and evaluation criteria. Additionally, it should be noted how agencies do , in fact, successfully collaborate and forge policy partnerships to strengthen a diversified ecosystem of entrepreneurial assistance.

It should be noted that EDA plays a key role in leading and shaping federal policy for fostering collaborative economic development. In this leadership role, EDA has built upon its long practice of coordinating with other federal agencies and its knowledge of best practices in economic development to create new initiatives designed to more strategically advance collaborative regional economic development. These initiatives formally leverage each partner's complementary activities to advance regional economic development activity, including infrastructure, entrepreneurial talent, technology, business incubation, best management practices, and access to capital. For example, recent inter-agency collaborative efforts include initiatives such as the Jobs and Innovation Accelerator Challenges (e.g., Advanced Manufacturing and Rural Jobs and Innovation Accelerators); i6 Challenge, i6 Green Challenge, Energy Regional Innovation Cluster Initiative, and the Strong Cities Strong Communities (SC2) Challenge. These initiatives represent EDA's commitment to tearing down "silos" across federal agencies (reducing fragmentation), significantly lessening the burden on grant applicants applying for funding from multiple federal sources (eliminating duplication), and jointly directing federal resources towards projects that advance common goals and objectives of each agency (mitigating overlap).

In the first Jobs and Innovation Accelerator Challenge (FY 2011), for example, EDA worked with the Department of Labor and the Small Business Administration to develop a streamlined application process in order to award 20 grants to organizations proposing to provide business assistance, employment training, and support for regional innovation clusters as part of an overall collaborative effort, but where each funding agency supported unique projects with discrete goals and objectives that aligned with the unique goals of each respective agency. Similar recent initiatives have also seen EDA partner with the Department of Agriculture, the Department of Energy, the Department of Labor, the National Institute of Standards and Technology, and the National Science Foundation. These efforts have enabled EDA and its funding agency partners to create an efficient selection process that decreases the burden borne by applicants, while collectively investing in projects that further commonly-held agency goals.

In terms of information tracking and performance measurement, EDA has established performance measures for each of its programs; namely, EDA tracks the number of jobs created and private investment leveraged for each construction project it funds. These performance measurements are subject to thorough review and validation procedures, are reported in the agency's annual report to Congress, and comply with the Government Performance and Results Act (GPRA). In addition to these outcome measures, EDA closely monitors outputs and administrative processes to better assess the efficacy of its

programs. Similarly, EDA routinely conducts evaluations of its programs (often limited
only by lack of resources), both internally, and through third-party research, and makes
available the findings of such evaluations (Note: EDA's performance metrics were
founded on an independent study of investments carried out by Rutgers in 1996. This
study was updated and validated in 2008 through a separate study conducted by Grant
Thornton.

Though EDA continually seeks to bolster and enhance the quality and quantity of its
performance metrics and evaluative capacity, the agency has a well-documented history
of commitment to program evaluation and measurement. EDA agrees with GAO's focus
on the need for more specific, focused information tracking and more frequent
performance evaluation broadly; however, many of the general statements about the need
for additional work in this area seem to be a result of the fact that efforts to track and
monitor project progress seem to have been outside the scope of the report. This broad
statement affords little to policy design and development. EDA agrees that additional
attention should be examined in this area, and encourages GAO to conduct an analysis
and identify best practices and methodologies on evaluation and performance
management that could be utilized more strategically to inform Congress and federal
agencies.

Appendix VIII: Comments from the Department of Housing and Urban Development

U.S. DEPARTMENT OF HOUSING AND URBAN DEVELOPMENT
WASHINGTON, DC 20410-5000

ASSISTANT SECRETARY FOR
PUBLIC AND INDIAN HOUSING

AUG 1 0 2012

Mr. William B. Shear, Director
Financial Markets and Community Investment
U.S. Government Accountability Office
411 G Street, NW
Washington, DC 20548

Dear Mr. Shear:

The Department of Housing and Urban Development's Office of Public and Indian Housing has reviewed the draft report on *Entrepreneurial Assistance: Opportunities Exist to Improve Programs' Collaboration, Data-Tracking, and Performance Management (#250601)*. Thank you for the opportunity to comment.

I am concerned that the Indian Community Development Block Grant (ICDBG) program is featured prominently on the first page of the report as one of 19 economic development programs that failed to meet their entrepreneurial performance goals. I am requesting that the statement be modified, so that the entire program is not unfairly perceived as ineffective.

HUD contends the draft report misrepresents ICDBG as an economic development program. The ICDBG is a relatively small program that mainly focuses on community development. While economic development is an eligible ICDBG activity, it represents only 3 percent of all projects funded since 2005. Of the $482,445,267 awarded for ICDBG during this time, only $16,914,999 (3.5 percent) funded economic development activities. Most ICDBG grants are used for building community buildings, developing infrastructure of various types, and rehabilitating housing units on Indian lands.

As stated in the GAO report, the study's focus is economic development programs that support entrepreneurs. HUD feels, given the ICDBG's focus on community development and its relatively small percentage of economic development activity, specifically emphasizing the ICDBG program on the first page overstates the role the program has in economic development – especially when there are many other programs referred to in the study that could be named instead of the ICDBG program.

The ICDBG program is a statutory set-aside of the much larger, formula-driven Community Development Block Grant program. ICDBG grants are awarded in response to an annual program Notice of Funding Availability, and applications are very competitive.

A comprehensive independent evaluation of the ICDBG program was conducted in 2006, at the request of the Office of Management and Budget. Econometrica, Inc. performed the evaluation. The evaluators found that a high proportion of the funds are awarded for community infrastructure projects. Specifically the report said:

www.hud.gov   espanol.hud.gov

2

- "ICDBG grants primarily funded activities to improve the social viability of the reservation communities and secondarily to enhance economic viability. ICDBG projects that improved social viability included health clinics and multipurpose community centers. Significant amounts of grant funds also were used for basic infrastructure projects to enhance the livability of housing and the operation of public facilities."

- "The employment benefits of ICDBG projects appeared to be a secondary priority for most sites we visited. Instead, grantees are devoting their ICDBG leveraged funds to projects that meet basic human needs, such as health, nutrition, infrastructure, and housing. While ICDBG projects do provide employment, almost all these positions are with tribal governments or agencies. In the ICDBG program, there has been only a limited focus on developing commercial or industrial entities that generate employment opportunities and revenues for the tribe."

HUD supports efforts to accurately measure the performance of its programs. In fact, the Office of Native American Programs (ONAP), which is a division within Public and Indian Housing, has recognized the limitations in its method of projecting and measuring performance in the ICDBG program. Earlier this year, ONAP began drafting a revised form to be used at grant application and at grant closeout to better collect performance measurement data. ONAP is also examining its data collection procedures as well as the methodology used to establish program targets.

As many tribal leaders and beneficiaries will attest, the ICDBG program addresses many important community development goals beyond those measured in the report. The program should not in any way be characterized as a failure, especially based on an analysis of fewer than 3 percent of the program's projects. ICDBG's reputation as a successful and important program in Indian Country should not be compromised by such a relatively minor flaw in its performance measurement process. Thank you for your thoughtful consideration.

Sincerely,

Sandra B. Henriquez
Assistant Secretary

Appendix XI: GAO Contact and Staff Acknowledgments

GAO Contact	William B. Shear, (202) 512-8678 or shearw@gao.gov.
Staff Acknowledgments	In addition to the contact named above, Marshall Hamlett and Triana McNeil (Assistant Directors), Matthew Alemu, Ben Bolitzer, Julianne Dieterich, Cindy Gilbert, Geoffrey King, Terence Lam, Alma Laris, Marc Molino, Alise Nacson, Jennifer Schwartz, and Karen Villafana made key contributions to this report.

GAO's Mission	The Government Accountability Office, the audit, evaluation, and investigative arm of Congress, exists to support Congress in meeting its constitutional responsibilities and to help improve the performance and accountability of the federal government for the American people. GAO examines the use of public funds; evaluates federal programs and policies; and provides analyses, recommendations, and other assistance to help Congress make informed oversight, policy, and funding decisions. GAO's commitment to good government is reflected in its core values of accountability, integrity, and reliability.
Obtaining Copies of GAO Reports and Testimony	The fastest and easiest way to obtain copies of GAO documents at no cost is through GAO's website (www.gao.gov). Each weekday afternoon, GAO posts on its website newly released reports, testimony, and correspondence. To have GAO e-mail you a list of newly posted products, go to www.gao.gov and select "E-mail Updates."
Order by Phone	The price of each GAO publication reflects GAO's actual cost of production and distribution and depends on the number of pages in the publication and whether the publication is printed in color or black and white. Pricing and ordering information is posted on GAO's website, http://www.gao.gov/ordering.htm. Place orders by calling (202) 512-6000, toll free (866) 801-7077, or TDD (202) 512-2537. Orders may be paid for using American Express, Discover Card, MasterCard, Visa, check, or money order. Call for additional information.
Connect with GAO	Connect with GAO on Facebook, Flickr, Twitter, and YouTube. Subscribe to our RSS Feeds or E-mail Updates. Listen to our Podcasts. Visit GAO on the web at www.gao.gov.
To Report Fraud, Waste, and Abuse in Federal Programs	Contact: Website: www.gao.gov/fraudnet/fraudnet.htm E-mail: fraudnet@gao.gov Automated answering system: (800) 424-5454 or (202) 512-7470
Congressional Relations	Katherine Siggerud, Managing Director, siggerudk@gao.gov, (202) 512-4400, U.S. Government Accountability Office, 441 G Street NW, Room 7125, Washington, DC 20548
Public Affairs	Chuck Young, Managing Director, youngc1@gao.gov, (202) 512-4800 U.S. Government Accountability Office, 441 G Street NW, Room 7149 Washington, DC 20548

Please Print on Recycled Paper.

www.ingramcontent.com/pod-product-compliance
Lightning Source LLC
Chambersburg PA
CBHW081111290526

45795CB00006B/2088